UP THE HILL TO BAKER RIVER SCHOOL

First published by Dog Ear Publishing
4010 W. 86th Street, Ste H
Indianapolis, IN 46268
www.dogearpublishing.net

ISBN: 978-160844-387-1

This book is printed on acid-free paper.

Printed in the United States of America

TABLE OF CONTENTS

PART ONE:
GROWING UP IN THE DARKNESS - NOT BEING ENOUGH

PART TWO -
MOVING INTO THE LIGHT – FINDING MYSELF

PART THREE -
THE BUTTERFLY EMERGES

PART FOUR -
THE CLOSING OF BAKER RIVER SCHOOL

Women's stories have not been told. And without stories there is no articulation of experience. Without stories a woman is lost when she comes to make the important decisions of her life. She does not learn to value her struggles, to celebrate her strengths, to comprehend her pain. Without stories she is alienated from those deeper experiences of self and world that have been called spiritual or religious. She is closed in silence. The expression of women's spiritual quest is integrally related to the telling of women's stories. If women's stories are not told, the depth of women's souls will not be known.

Carol Christ, *Diving Deep and Surfacing*

PREFACE

A Message to the Entire Baker River School Community:

Baker River School became a reality as the result of the participation, commitment, support and endeavor of many people, which included staff, students, parents and friends. As a personal memoir, this book recounts what I recall as having most personal impact for me. It makes no attempt at a systematic history, chronicle of events or inclusion of the names of many who had significant roles in the school's creation and operation. Please know that I am deeply aware of and grateful for the very significant contributions so many of you made, and also how different your stories of "how it really was" might be from what I have told here. Whatever the "truth" might be for each of you, I want you to know that without you there would simply not have been any school to remember and write about.

A Message to My Children Sally, Berit and Sam

I also imagine that your memories may be very different from those related in my story, especially yours, Sam. You were impacted most by our decision to start our own school. At age 12, your reasonably normal life of home, neighbors, best friends, baseball league, and summer camp was interrupted for an atypical lifestyle of homeschooling in 1974, something unheard of in our community. From that, you went, with us, to living in a 25-foot trailer for a year traveling around the United States in 1976-77. A year later you went with us to create Baker River School, which became your home as well. In retrospect, I understand that my passion and enthusiasm for starting both the Hobbit (my home school) and Baker River School may have been more about my reaction to my own childhood experience than your need. Although the school served many young people as school and home-away-from-home, I imagine your experience was unique.

And you too, Bent and Sally, each contributed in significant ways to the life of the school.

You are all now adults with children of your own. We have loved watching you evolve into your roles as partners and parents and professionals. Who knows? Maybe someday you, as well as other students and staff, will write your own Baker River School stories.

A Message to My Parents

Mom and dad, this memoir is not meant to blame you or your parenting. In many ways you gave me so much to be grateful for: a beautiful home to grow up in, the luxury of two months of summer camp for eight summers in New Hampshire, a far better educational opportunity than women in previous generations received, family trips and vacations, and a peaceful, safe environment. Writing this memoir is about understanding myself and how I interpreted my childhood relationships with you and others and childhood events in a way that did not allow me to complete my growing up. I know that you gave me what you could emotionally and intellectually, based partly on what you did or didn't receive in your own childhood families. You never withheld anything from me intentionally. Whatever resentment I harbored over the years or blamed you for that shows up in this memoir has now been now replaced with understanding. My love and gratefulness flow to you. Thank you wherever you are. I feel a deep sense of gratitude for you as my parents and I am deeply grateful for my life.

APPRECIATIONS

To my husband Bruce not only for his role in making Baker River School happen but for his unrelenting support and patience in making this book happen. On many occasions, when my patience with my limited computer skills had reached the end, and I was ready to throw the computer out the window along with the book, he was there to find the lost piece of writing, or show me the technology needed to take the next step and keep on moving. And then for his total support in proofreading the manuscript many times and putting to work his English teacher's expertise and skills in grammar, spelling, sentence structure, and style. This is his book also.

To Cindy Barrilleaux, for editing the book (what a job that was!) and for being the writing teacher who convinced me I could write a book in the first place. You helped me to get started by filling my cup with validations and appreciations, a huge contradiction to everything I learned growing up.

To Ash Eames, who was the first to tackle the initial manuscript and go through it page by page writing helpful comments and making corrections everywhere. Ash was also an important part of BRS having been on the staff for the last two years besides being an old friend to both Bruce and me.

PART ONE:

GROWING UP IN SILENCE

Chapter One

MY FATHER

In June 1977, before my husband Bruce and I rented what came to be called the Yellow House and planned the opening of Baker River School in Wentworth, New Hampshire, my father died at the age of 79. I was 45, married 22 years, with three children.

I was actually relieved when my mother notified me of his death. No longer did I have to feel that same obligation to visit him that I had felt as a child, having to kiss him good night every night. I had experienced him as not showing much interest in me back then, and nothing had changed over the years. The hope for his affection that I had clung to as a child had died long before he did.

About a week after my father died, my mother found four letters in his safe deposit box, one for each of his three daughters and one to my mother. I don't know what he said to the others. True to form, we never discussed the letters with each other. But in his letter to me were the words I had longed to hear him speak to me my whole life: "I love you so much."

I was stunned and then angry. Now he was telling me how much he loved me and how special I was to him! Why could he never speak these words? And how often had he felt these feelings but couldn't find the words to express them? Now he was gone, and we would never tell each other about our love for each other.

My father was an honest, gentle, kind man. He had begun his own business in New York City in 1933 after he had lost his job and all his money during The Great Depression. The business was very successful and he was loved and respected by his many professional friends. I believe his value and worth as a human being came through his success as a newspaper publisher. I often describe his work as his fourth and most beloved child. He lived through his work.

Shortly after World War II ended he adopted a war orphan named Moritz Markovitz from Poland, and every month he would send him money and write a long letter to him telling him about our family and how he wanted to help Moritz with his education and getting a job. He insisted that the whole family write to him also which we did. He was also attentive to young men in this country who were just beginning their careers in business and would coach them endlessly. He was a business coach before coaching became a profession.

I was born in 1932 and thus grew up in the '30s and '40's. My family was very kind and polite, and its behavior was very predictable: an upper-middle class, privileged family in an affluent New Jersey community. There was no violence or abuse. My parents were good people. But it was a "How-are-you-fine" kind of family, lacking any emotional vocabulary. Feelings were avoided.

The family house on Elston Road was built in 1927. Elston Road was a quiet neighborhood street, lined on both sides with large maple and sycamore trees. In the hot summer months, the trees formed an arch over the street providing us with the needed shade from the sometimes scorching sun. My best friend Maryanne lived next door, and the path from my front door to hers was well worn. She was beautiful and smart, and like a sister. I could turn to her for help with my homework. In our teens, she was the one I confided to on the subject of dating and boyfriends.

Dinner was served every night at seven in our formal dining room. The table was set with a lace table cloth, fine china and two lighted candelabras. I liked to flatten the hot, smooth melting wax as it dripped down the sides of the candelabras until one night my mother pointed out in her refined voice that my hands belonged in my lap unless I was eating. From then on I just watched the wax as it formed patterns down the sides of the crystal.

The conversations at dinner were mostly between my sisters and my father. My sister Sally, the middle daughter, loved to argue about politics, although arguments were referred to as debates or discussions. Sometimes my father would complain about his day in New York City and something his boss had said that angered my father. My mother always answered, "Oh Morse, that's terrible." She always supported him. I would just watch and listen. Nobody asked me any questions. All the conversations stayed on the surface.

Ada, our maid, would go back and forth through the swinging door from the kitchen to the dining room to serve the meal, wearing a starched white uniform and clean white apron. I loved Ada. She asked me more questions about my life than anyone in my family. In my teens, she insisted on knowing about my boyfriends and who I was dating. In hindsight, I think she may have realized I had no one to talk to, and stepped in to fill the void in my life.

My father served the main course, carving, for example, a roast beef from his place at the head of the table. Ada would take each plate and circle the table placing a plate in front of each one of us. My mother was always served first and as the youngest I was always served last. After everyone had been served the meat, Ada would leave and reappear with the second item on the menu, vegetables, or potatoes, or rice, and so forth until our plates were filled and we could begin to eat.

Thursday night was Ada's night off, so we ate in the kitchen and my mother prepared the meal. The main dish was usually the roast beef from the night before sliced and served cold with hot gravy.

My mother came from an affluent family and with servants to prepare meals, so she grew up with little confidence in her cooking. Her sole specialty was popover muffins and when the muffins came out of the oven fully "popped", I could see the sense of relief on her face.

Sunday night was also her night to cook, and my sisters and I were responsible for cleaning up. We often argued over whose night it was to wash the dishes. If we couldn't settle the argument, we would call in mom to mediate. She was gentle and kind, and never raised her voice or showed any anger towards us. She would go out of her way never to show partiality towards us. Even at Christmas she made sure that we all received the same number of presents.

Everything was predictable in my house. I was a poor student, receiving mostly C's and C-pluses, and sometimes an incomplete, as was the case in eighth grade math. Actually, I hated school, but I adapted out of necessity. But I couldn't not go to school. I needed the contact with my friends. And besides, there was nothing to do at home. What I was reading or learning did not arouse any curiosity in me. School was a place where I was expected to go to five days a week. My parents never asked me any questions about school or checked up on my school work. An incomplete in math received no attention. And I never thought to ask them for help.

Our house was cleaned every day and was always in perfect order. You would never know that three children lived in the house. Our toys stayed in our rooms, where we spent most of our time. Jay, my oldest sister by four years, kept the door to her room closed. The message was, "Stay out"! The love of her life was horses. Her bed and bedroom chair were covered with soft, furry stuffed horses as well as more fragile pottery horses on display on a shelf over her bureau. Being the oldest, she had the largest room in the front of the house across from my parent's bedroom.

Sally was eighteen months older than I. Our bedrooms were in the rear of the house, close to each other. We liked to play with our dolls, and for awhile we kept a scrap book of pictures of beautiful babies, which we would cut out of old magazines my mother saved. At another time, we collected pictures of princesses. Princess Elizabeth of England was our favorite.

I was in awe of my sisters. Jay not only rode horses but jumped horses. When she was fifteen she was a member of the Montclair Mounted Troop, a junior drill team which met one afternoon a week in the winter. I loved to go with my mother to pick her up after practice and on some days to arrive early enough to watch the riders on their horses maneuver the different patterns like those of a marching band. Watching her ride was a thrill. Sally was inspiring to me for totally different reasons, but what I remember the most was that she was skinny. She had the tiny waist, thin hips, and a beautiful turned up nose I always wanted to have. I was the pudgy one. My childhood pictures as a chubby baby were often pointed out with laughter that was meant in fun but I took the message to heart. I grew up seeing myself as fat and unconsciously compared myself to her. I spent hours standing in front of the hall mirror looking at myself from all angles, trying on clothes that would hide what I didn't like and in fact despised.

As the youngest, I had the smallest room and my clothes and bedroom furniture were handed down from my sisters. I loved their clothes because I imagined myself as older and more mature in them! I always wanted to be more grown up like them. My dolls were my main focus. When I was in elementary school, I spent a great deal of time playing with them, putting them to bed at night and waking them up in the morning, dressing them and undressing them, talking to them like a mother talks to her children. I even had my own 6'x 8' play house in the back yard. Eventually I brought my dolls and doll furniture from my bedroom out there and even sewed curtains to fit the windows.

Our back yard was divided into two yards separated by a tall hedge. My mother loved to garden so on one side of the hedge were her gardens and on the other side was a play yard. She spent many hours weeding and tending to her flowers. I planted a flower garden next to the little porch in the front of my playhouse. I knew at a very young age that when I grew up I would be a mother and a housewife like my mother. I certainly didn't aspire to being a school teacher, and would never have dreamed I would create and run schools! Later on, as dolls became less of an interest for me, the playhouse became more of a club house for me and my friends.

Eventually, my interests turned to boys, an interest which became an obsession.

Like most girls, I believed that not having a date was a reflection of whether I was pretty enough. There was shame about not having a date. Being popular, not smart, was my goal. That, I thought, was how I would eventually meet my life partner and live happily ever after. Little did I know!

I grew up trying to be a good girl, to do as I was told by my parents. I was sure that their love for me was dependent on that. They rewarded my good behavior with presents, like my beloved, jet black, English bicycle with hand brakes, which my parents gave me one Christmas. I rode that bike to junior high school every day for three years, proud of the hand brakes, which I saw as a status symbol. Sweets, desserts and afternoon snacks made me feel loved, too. The first thing I would do when I came home from school in the afternoon was to go to the pantry and dip my hand into the cookie jar and pull out one of Ada's warm fresh-out-of-the-oven cookies or brownies.

My parents were well-meaning people. Since they had grown up in the same emotional void there was no way they could have known how utterly empty I felt inside. Since they never asked me what I was thinking or feeling, I didn't have the words to describe the emptiness. Outwardly, I pretended I was happy. But my experiences at school and with my parents fed my growing fears that I was not important, or loved, or smart.

Every weekday night after dinner and after playing with the dogs, my father would settle down into his chair in the sun room and read his business magazines cover to cover until he went to bed around

11:00. This was his ritual. He was the only family member who had his own chair. "That's your father's chair", I was told if I just happened to be sitting in it when he came into the room.

Often I walked up our tree-lined street to meet my dad at the local train station when he was coming home from a day in New York City. I always held the expectation that he would be excited to see me as I stood there on the platform and waved to him as he got off the train. I hoped he would wave back and welcome me with open arms, toss me around, tickle me, make me laugh, and show me off to the other dads. But it was always the same dad. He would greet me with a kiss on the forehead and silence. "Aren't you glad to see me?" I would think. "Look, I'm the only daughter here to greet their dad? Don't you see how good I am? Don't I make you happy?"

Our home was a short walk from the station. On the way he rarely asked me questions. But when we walked through our front door and when our dogs, Margie and Charlie, greeted him, he came alive. His face lit up. I would sit on the bottom step of the stairs watching him play and wondered how I could get him to like me as much as the dogs. At some point I decided I was the problem, because no matter what I did, I wasn't enough.

While he was downstairs after dinner reading his magazines every night, the rest of the family would be upstairs, everyone in their own room doing their homework or listening to the Lone Ranger, or Henry Aldrich or Blondie on their radios. No one, including my mother, came into my room to check up on homework or ask how my day went, and how school was, whether I needed help with my homework, or to even look at my homework.

Then, before I went to bed, I would faithfully go downstairs and kiss my dad good night. I felt no connection to him, but I felt obliged to do this ritual every night. Maybe, this ritual had started in hopes he would love me back. Or maybe I had hoped to learn to love him if I kissed him every night. Eventually I began to feel resentful when I got very little response coming from him. Some nights, though, I would be in bed, and ready to fall asleep, when this gnawing sense of guilt would creep in as I remembered I had not kissed him good night. I would reluctantly get out of bed and head down the darkened second floor hall, and down the stairs to the even darker front hall. There I would be guided by the light from the sunroom where he sat in "his" chair. He would be sitting all alone, with just the light from floor lamp next to his chair.

Everything in our home centered on my father's comfort. Nothing was expected of him. Once I happened to be walking through the kitchen when he had to get his own lunch. He was heating up an unopened can of soup in a pan of hot water!

In those days, men were not expected to cook or to even know anything about the kitchen much less food. That was a women's job. When my mother didn't get up to make his breakfast, I would stop what I was doing to get ready for school and hurry down to the kitchen to scramble his egg and make the coffee for him. I never saw him wash a dish, clear or clean off a table, do the laundry, sweep the floor or do anything that was in the remotest considered housework. Home was his hotel and the rest of the family were his servants.

My mother actually did practically nothing in the way of housework either. Ada cooked and took care of the kitchen. My mother ordered the food by phone and it was delivered a few hours later. Mary Greyboszki came to the house two days a week to attend to the laundry and ironing and clean the entire house.

My father once told my mother that the house reminded him of a museum. Was that a criticism of my mother's standards? Did he really see how many people were working to keep this place comfortable and relaxing for him? Or was he unable to say thank you everybody for making my life at home so special? Perhaps it was just another huge gap in his ability to express his feelings or gratitude or even see his home outside his needs. He knew nothing about how to take care of himself emotionally, or what his needs were, or what the needs of children were or how to run a house or be in relationships. I guess that was my image of all men. Real men lived outside the home, on the golf course or in their offices.

Because my father was so loved and admired by his friends and business associates, and even by my friends, at some point in my formative years I convinced myself that I loved him, although in my heart, he felt like a stranger. I resented him, and then felt guilty. How could I have negative feelings when he is working so hard to bring home the money and support the family!?! I wanted to adore him. And I wanted him to adore me. So I pretended to adore him and act on that.

Chapter Two

MY MOTHER

"I didn't take it! I didn't take it! I didn't take it!" I was five years old, sitting on the fancy canopy bed in their bedroom. My mother was repeatedly accusing me of taking a ten dollar bill from her dresser, probably thinking I wanted play money when I played house with my dolls. She wouldn't believe that I hadn't taken it. She had put me on a high bed to confront me and break me down to confessing the truth. My oldest sister Jay stood on one side of the bed. And my other sister Sally stood on the other side. My mother stood at the end of the bed. No escaping, I was surrounded.

My father was the only one not there. He was at work in New York City as usual. The year was 1938. Even though my father had successfully gone back to work a few years earlier, in the depths of The Great Depression, money was still very precious. Ten dollars was a lot of money. I could hear the fear in my mother's voice: she wanted to find that money. Perfect play money, she must have thought. "She took it to use playing house. Perfect motive." She wasn't raising her voice but the more I said, "No I didn't", the more she launched into, "So where did you put it?" "I didn't take it", I would plead back to her.

Eventually, when I realized she would never believe me, I started naming places I had put it: in the leaf pile under the grate next to the cellar window, I'd say.   And she would send Jay or Sally to investigate and see if the money was there, while I just kept thinking to myself a string of reactions. "Why me? How about my sisters? Or why not the maid, Viola?   Don't you think I'm old enough to know whether I took it or not?   Why would you even think I was lying?   Do you really think I'm dishonest?   I mean do you really think that since you are making such a big deal of this, some memory of having taken the money wouldn't come back to me, at least remember reaching up to the top of your dresser and delighting in finding this play money?   If I had the money or knew where it was, what would be my motive for not telling you, not just running off to my doll house or wherever the money was, and just giving it to you, especially since you don't seem to be angry?"

So the process continued. Sally or Jay would return and report the money wasn't in the leaf pile, which of course I knew it wasn't. Then she would ask me again. "Where did you put the money?" I resorted to lying and making up as many other places as I could think of where the money might be, continuing to know that I hadn't put it there.

Perhaps by then I was beginning to doubt myself. "Maybe I did take the money. After all, this is my mother and she should know. Maybe I am lying to myself about not having taken the money." Maybe sitting there on top of that big bed surrounded by my family, I stopped believing in myself and believing them. Maybe I had taken it. Since no one else believes me, maybe I couldn't believe myself.

I don't remember at what point the interrogation ended or when my mother gave up. I just know I never got any reassurance or apology. Nothing like"I'm sorry to have put you through that."

My mother was essentially kind and soft spoken. In my anxiety and fear of being alone, my connection to her was comforting. But at a very deep emotional level, I suspect my connection to her was not based on a healthy attachment to her. The feeling of separation was huge, and some of my life experiences later on at critical times in my life revealed even more deeply that disconnection.

I never knew much about my mother's childhood. It wasn't until I was in my forties that I learned about the tragic death of her baby sister, Ruth. I have a photograph of mom and her sister just before Ruth died. Mom was six years old. The picture showed her gently touching the face of her three year old sister. They looked so happy, in beautiful white dresses with white buttons up the front and high collars, petticoats, and high-topped laced black shoes. They each wore a locket around their neck.

One day soon after the picture was taken, Ruth got the measles, and a few nights later Ruth died. Mom had just recovered from measles herself.

I wonder who was there with her when she heard Ruth crying out in the night in the room next to hers. Where was my grandmother? And who was with Ruth? And who comforted my mom and rocked her and held her through her grief? Did she perhaps believe she was responsible for her little sister's death because Ruth caught the measles from her? Did anyone ask her?

And what did mom feel when her mother dressed Ruth in her white dress with buttons and laid her dead body out on the couch as was the tradition then? And how would this event affect her when she became the mother of three little girls?

I wish I knew.

Many years later, when mom was diagnosed with terminal cancer, my sister Sally and her family took her into their home. When I visited her in her last days, I wanted to have the conversations with her that we had never had. I wanted to ask her how she felt about death. Did she know she was dying and did she want to talk about it? Did she want to talk about her life? About my father, about being a mother or about being a grandmother? Did she want to talk about Ruth?

But as I sat there beside her watching her sleep, I realized I couldn't ask her any of those questions. I was frozen in my own fear: fear that my questions would raise her feelings and upset her and the rest of the family rather than bring us closer together: fear of breaking the code of silence in the family. The emotional distance between my mother and me would have to live on.

Mom died in 1987 at the age of 87, ten years after my father's death. I remember crying at the shock of hearing my sister tell me that she had died. I couldn't believe it. But I don't remember feeling sad, maybe more relieved than anything. A few years later, I was helping a friend grieve the death of her mom, and I wondered if I had grieved the death of my mom. I still don't know.

Chapter Three

SCHOOL

My grade school felt like a cage to me. I was bored and unmotivated. I just didn't see why I should be there. I hated school. I spent more time focused on the big clock above the door than on any place else in the room. My seventh grade classroom was dark, with old faded pictures on the walls of old men with beards and grey hair, and wearing old-fashioned suits. My seat was right underneath the window and when I wasn't looking at the clock, I was gazing out the window, watching the birds in the trees and calculating how long it would be before I could get on my bike and head home for lunch. I imagined being a bird and how much fun it would be to swing on branches and fly, and swing and fly, all day long. I wanted that freedom.

One day stands out in my memory from all the rest. Mr. Flynn, the only male teacher in the school, was standing in front of the room dressed in his usual black suit and green tie and black shoes. I didn't feel well, kind of sick to my stomach. I raised my hand and asked if I could be excused. He gave me a nod of approval and I quickly went to the girls' room. As soon as the door closed to the bathroom, I began to sob. I couldn't stop. One of my sister's best friends came into the room and asked me what was wrong. Having learned in my family to control my tears so I wouldn't be called a "cry baby", I gathered up control to stop the crying, and simply said, "I don't know. I don't feel well".

She took me by the hand in a very motherly way and walked me down the hall to the principal's office. This felt like a very scary place to be, because I didn't want to throw up here either, let alone cry in front of this man. He would probably hate me if I did that. Everyone in the whole school would hear about it and then I wouldn't have any friends. I wanted Alice to stay with me and keep holding my hand but she had to leave. I felt no connection or empathy from him. Just a very matter-of-fact statement of the school procedure with student illness. He called my mother and shortly afterwards she came rushing into his office, probably to make sure I was not dying. She always panicked when one of us three kids got sick.

I held back the tears until we were alone in the car. Then through the tears I told her, "I don't know what is wrong." By this time, I felt not so much like throwing up but a deep, deep feeling of emptiness and longing and need to cling to her. I had no language to describe the feeling, and she seemed to have no idea of how to help me. For the next two weeks I cried every morning and refused to go to school because I couldn't tolerate being away from my mother. I was like a newborn, needing constant holding, nourishment and attention. I couldn't leave her side. Home was the only place that felt safe. My father worked at home until after lunch and then headed for his office in the city. But he never asked me why I was home or how I felt. No one in my family asked me about school, about my life, about my friends, about Mr. Flynn, about what I loved or what I hated, or about any fears I had or even something as simple as "What did you do yesterday? Or "What did you like about today?" And no one in my family cried, except me.

Was anyone trying to figure me out? Find out what was wrong? I didn't know. Did they see me as sick? I wanted to know what was wrong with me. Sometimes I'd lie in my bed, thinking: someone talk to me; someone ask me a question." But I didn't dare voice those thoughts. I hated the need to cling to my mom. I hated following her around everywhere and the panicky feeling I had waiting for her to come home if she went some place.

Eventually I recovered on my own and within a few weeks I returned to school and sat in the same seat I had sat in a few weeks ago, still looking out the window wishing I were somewhere else. I concluded that it was natural to hate school. I passed tests by memorizing facts that I would forget a few days after the test. School was about grades only. I never expected school could be interesting, let alone thrilling. I certainly didn't think it could be a place for emotional connection and healing. But then, that was decades before my transformation and Baker River School. I simply knew that school did not figure into my future.

In my teens, like most girls, I was preoccupied with boys and obsessed with who liked me and who didn't. In that era, it was inevitable that I would look forward to being a wife and mother, because that's what women did. I knew that only my husband's grades mattered, because he was the one who would be working. Being smart might be important for a good job but not for me as a wife and mother. My graduating from college was important for the reputation of the family and was an indication of the success of my parents. And it never occurred to me that I had the option of not going to college - I wouldn't want to disappoint or displease my parents in that way.

Both of my sisters, after four years of college, went to Katherine Gibbs Secretarial School for a year at the insistence of my father. He said he was preparing them for a job market which basically limited women's possibilities to being secretaries, teachers, or nurses. It was understood that even those jobs would end as soon as we found husbands. Then, we could begin our true careers as a wife and mother. Of course, nothing I learned in college prepared me for that role.

My internal emptiness continued throughout my childhood and adolescence. I learned not to let people know, because the message was clear: my "sensitivity" was the problem. So I grew up feeling like the oddball in the family. Rather than be different, I was careful when I cried, to go to my one safe haven, my room, so no one would know.

Chapter Four

MY FATHER MEETS BRUCE

In June 1955 I proudly returned home from college graduation wearing Bruce's fraternity pin. I had never felt so excited. Maybe I had felt depressed my whole childhood. Being with Bruce liberated me from the trapped feeling of being alone and feeling empty. I finally felt connected.

I had met Bruce on a blind date the last few months of college. He was the first person who ever told me he loved me. I had never heard those words spoken by my parents, although I know they loved me. In high school, any boy who was attracted to me was in a no-win situation. If he pursued me, calling me frequently, or driving by my house and honking the horn, or wanting to pick me up from school, my attraction soon faded. Being pursued felt smothering and unfamiliar to me. The boys I was attracted to were the ones that didn't call me, didn't seek me out. If they showed no interest in me, like my dad, their unavailability got my attention.

Bruce fit into this category in some ways. Emotionally, he was somewhat distant like my father. I was attracted to his intelligence and his emotional distance. I didn't care that he didn't seek me out at parties. I wasn't bothered when he didn't show me attention. I was attracted to his independence. He was interesting, funny, listened well, and was smart. He could talk about any subject; sometimes I listened to him in awe as he talked to friends about politics, or the Boston Red Sox. With his social ease and intelligence, he had all those parts of me I felt were missing. When I was with him I felt whole. Our sexual connection was the proof I wanted that he loved me. We had chemistry, and I experienced at last that long sought-after bond to another person. What happened outside of our sex life didn't seem to matter until much later on in our marriage. I was confident that Bruce had all the credentials to meet my parent's concept of the ideal husband for me. His dad was a lawyer who attended Harvard Law School. His mother taught second grade. They were first generation Swedish. Altogether they were a beautiful family.

I called mom from Worcester, where I was visiting Bruce's family after his graduation from Dartmouth. I shared my good news and announced I had invited Bruce to come home with me for a few days before he had to report to Officers Candidate School (OCS) in Newport, Rhode Island. She sounded mildly excited. I told her we would be home by dinnertime.

As we walked through the front door, Ada was the first one to greet us. Shortly after I introduced her to him, she pulled me aside to tell me how handsome he was. My mother was very polite as usual, and I hoped excited, but she didn't show it.

The dinner scene that night was tense. Bruce was nervous meeting my family for the first time and so was I, knowing that I was in love with him and I wanted my family to love him also. I was sure once the conversation got going at dinner, they would find out more about him and love him too. So I had assured him my parents were very easy going and friendly with guests and there was nothing to worry about. I was therefore unprepared for the silence and cold shoulder my father gave to him.

My father had been in the navy in World War I and loved to talk about ships and being in the service. I was sure that would be a shared interest they could talk about. Despite knowing Bruce was about to go to OCS, my father never once asked him questions or volunteered information. Bruce might just as well not have been at the table, given the conversation. My father never as much as welcomed him to our home. I wondered if it was because Bruce and I were in love, and then I thought perhaps he had some prejudice against Swedes.

But in reality, it was just life as usual at my house. Once again I felt invisible to my father. This moment of a new beginning wasn't really happening or, if it was, it really wasn't very important. I had naively gotten my hopes up that I would receive some validation. I was furious and heartbroken at the silence, even though I should have known better.

When Bruce and I decided to marry, my mother told me in so many words that we shouldn't disturb my father with it. "We won't talk about the wedding in front of your father. All the plans will be just between you and me." The silence was painful and confusing to me. Months later, I wrote my father a letter that expressed my sadness.

> I remember hearing you say that what a girl feels or thinks is in their mother's department, but I am in total disagreement. What goes on in my life is just as much your department as mother's and you certainly must be concerned about the step I am taking which is the most important decision of my whole life. Being in love with Bruce has made me one of the happiest girls in the world and I want to be able to share that happiness with you and mother. It's a most saddening feeling to think that because I have fallen in love; my own father ignores me and acts totally uninterested or is maybe even mad at me. I've felt extremely hurt in the past 3 months and want more than anything else in the world for you to share this happiness with me and help me if maybe you think I am doing the wrong thing. Please try to understand all that I have said and instead of ignoring the whole thing, talk to me.

"Talk to me"….that's what I felt I had been saying to him my whole life. "Talk to me."

Much to my surprise and happiness, I received just the letter I needed and wanted back from him

> Dear Poochie, (*Note: his nickname for me*)
>
> You have written a wonderful letter, Bets, as only a gal like you could write and if you aren't sure of it, now let me assure you in every way that I can that there isn't anything that you have done or ever could do that would in any way affect my feelings toward you. In short….I'm in no way whatever mad, disappointed or what-have-you at you so have no worries on that score. You are still and always TOPS in my book, no matter what I say or how I "look."
>
> I haven't and will never attempt to tell any gals of mine who they should or shouldn't tie up with. I have full confidence in your own ability to pick the lad you should have. So if I have any question about the situation at all, it's entirely one of timing…of feeling that no youngsters should jump into a thing like this too quickly and without time to realize the responsibilities that come with it. This in no ways concerns your selection of Bruce.
>
> You are the best, Bets, so don't worry about anything as far as I'm concerned. Just have fun and be sure that's the mostest that I want for you.
>
> We can talk about this some more when I get home, if you like, but meanwhile turn off your "worrier" and enjoy yourself. Pop

I thought the silence was over, but when he arrived home, we both slipped back to where we had been. And I did not know how to talk to him.

Bruce and I were married the following April, with never a conversation between me and my dad. He walked me down the aisle, but giving away the bride was an empty ritual. I felt no connection. The next day Bruce and I left for California. I don't remember even saying good bye to my parents.

When I called home a few months later to announce I was pregnant, my father answered the phone. All he said was, "Oh my God." I hung up on him and gave up on him.

The world of emotional silence my parents grew up in had profound effects on me as their daughter. And for me as a mother. Years later, I would finally find words for my emotions, and my passion would become helping young people and their parents learn the power and safety of emotional connections.

Chapter Six

BERIT'S BIRTH 1958

Over the next six years, we brought three children into the world: Sally in January 1957, Berit in July 1958 and Sam in November 1962. Sally was born while Bruce was in the Navy and we lived in California. Berit was born towards the end of his assignment on the USS Mathews, which was stationed in Long Beach, California, but spent much time deployed in the Far East. Just weeks before Berit's birth, he had been called home from Japan by the Red Cross to deal with an emergency family situation due to a sudden illness of his dad. At the same time he had been reassigned to Princeton University as an NROTC instructor, effective at the end of his emergency leave. At the time of Berit's birth he was attending to his family in Massachusetts, and I was living with my family in New Jersey.

The day of Berit's birth was July 11, 1958. My mother and father stood next to my hospital bed. I asked my mother to rub my back. She said she could for a few minutes but nothing longer because her broken toe was hurting. I asked my father for nothing. Unconsciously, I realized how little confidence he had in his ability to soothe me. That was a mom's job.

Only twenty-four hours before, on the operating table for a cae-sarean section, someone had botched the spinal and I had felt the knife slash into my uterus. When I screamed, the nurse slapped a mask over my nose and mouth. Shortly after the baby was safely out of the womb, they put me to sleep. Hours later I awoke from the nightmare, traumatized. It turned out that the spinal hadn't numbed the place of the knife's intrusion into my gut. The doctor came into my room and blamed me for the fiasco, accusing me of not telling him I had a crooked spine. The baby and I were both try-ing to survive the darkness of the moment.

Here is how I described the experience in a much later journal:

> The morning of your birth, I was filled with excitement and expectations that in the afternoon I would be holding you in my arms and welcoming you into the world. But here we are in this black hole now having to each pull our-selves out, me like a baby also with so little experience and understanding about life and how to be a Mother and who I am and what my purpose is and you, so fragile and dependent. Now the trauma is over but not the pain. You sleep alone in your crib in the hospital nursery with busy nurses rushing around you and bright lights shining down on you…no peace, no Mama to hold you and nurse you and rock you and talk to you and sleep by you. You are alone while I sleep down the hall in my beaten and bruised body. I feel overwhelmed. But what do we know of you, the baby who sleeps alone in your bassinet in the nursery. Someone go get the baby and bring her here. Wrap her in sweet smelling blankets from home and rock her and kiss her and hold her close and tell her all is well. You go get her, I wanted to tell my Mom. Then lay her beside me. Model your courage and strength for me. Look deep inside me right now, see my pain, see how much I need you right now so that I can mother my new baby. Stay with us. Be your wise powerful self.

Also much later, I re-read this entry at the time of learning about the death of my mother's baby sister, Ruth. It was at that time suddenly clear to me: what I wanted from my mom was exactly what my mom needed from her mom the night Ruth died. Instead, my mom's survival depended on telling herself that she did not need attention and could survive on her own. What she gave to me was what had been given to her. She grew up in the emotional void which carried over into our family. Once I understood that, I could forgive my mom, but this was many years later.

Chapter Six

THE HILL SCHOOL

After a five year stint in the navy, including two years of teaching at Princeton, Bruce got a job teaching at The Hill School, a traditional boys' secondary boarding school in Pottstown, Pennyslvania. We moved there in the fall of 1960 with our two very young daughters. The school was situated near the center of the town on top of a hill. A long winding driveway from the main street of town led to the formal campus with its imposing old buildings, traditional quadrangle, lush and well groomed lawns, and formal gardens. Dress at the school was formal, "coat-and-tie" with well-spelled out and detailed rules. This meant such requirements as pressed pants, tie and jacket, and soled-shoes for all academic and social appointments; and white collar dress shirt and tie shoes (no loafers) for Sunday meals and chapel. For the faculty wives, acceptable dress was nylons, a knee length dress or skirt and a loose, modest blouse.

It was a whole new world for me. Yet, as restrictive and forbidding as the Hill School was for faculty wives, in many ways my years living there were happy. I had many wonderful women friends. We relied on and took care of each other, and felt strong bonds not only to each other, but to each other's children. We were a community unto ourselves in an oppressive male community where women had their place and if they stepped out of it they were chastised. I seemed to always say the wrong thing and I would experience the repercussions.

Many things bothered me in regard to the way we were treated as faculty wives, including being strongly urged not to show up in the dining hall for our meals after we were seven months pregnant. The reason, we were told was, because one of the boys might by accident shove us against a table - boys will be boys. Since that made no sense to me, I concluded that the powers-that-be didn't like the way we looked shortly before giving birth.

The position of women in this small society was especially clear on the evening the poet Robert Frost was scheduled to give an informal talk to the faculty in the wood paneled faculty meeting room adjacent to the library. Wives were only allowed in this room by invitation, which usually entailed pouring tea and coffee. I had been asked to serve after Frost's talk, and I accepted. However, I was instructed not to ask any questions.

So on the evening of the event after Frost had given a more formal lecture to the whole school in Memorial Hall, I made my way up the formal staircase to the library on the second floor of this forbidding male-only building, tugging and straightening my dark blue knee-length high-neck wool dress with red trim around the waist and making last minute adjustments to my nylons and feeling for the clasp of my pearls, with great trepidation I entered the faculty lounge. Trying not to be seen, I slipped over to the table with its freshly ironed table cloth and polished-silver coffee urn surrounded by china saucers and cups. Liz, the other faculty wife who was given this assignment greeted me and we chatted quietly, all the while reminding myself not to speak but to pour the coffee or hot water for tea.

During the question and answer period, though, I had a burning question I wanted to ask Robert Frost. My heart was pounding. Voices in my head said, "Don't ask it, and don't ask it!" I ignored the voices and slowly raised my hand. Almost immediately, Mr. Frost nodded for me to go ahead with my question. I knew he had a summer home in Ripton, Vermont, where we had been going as a family for previous summers while Bruce was working on his MA degree at the Bread Loaf School of English. I asked about one of his poems and whether he was referring to one of the landmarks I had known in Ripton. He seemed to enjoy my question and talking about Ripton, a favorite place of his.

No one ever said anything to me about having spoken up, but I'm sure that later on there was chatter in the faculty mailroom. My main task was to be a servant not a thinker.

The headmaster and the "old guard" of the school were respectful and polite in the presence of the women, but their actions spoke louder than words. They might just as well have shouted, "Stick with your job and don't interfere with your husband's job. He is the intellectual and the one who counts here."

Betty Friedan's *The Feminine Mystique* came out during the time we lived at the Hill School. In it she captured perfectly the predominant attitude of men at the school: the women's movement was an insignificant nuisance about burning bras. It wouldn't be for another six years, after we'd moved away from The Hill, though, that her book would help revolutionize my thinking about myself.

Chapter Seven

SAM AND MISS PROWLEY

In the fall of 1969 we moved from The Hill School to West Boylston, Massachusetts. On the first day of school two years later, I was in the garage mixing paint when I glanced up and caught a glimpse of Sam, our nine year old third grader, walking toward the house slowly with his head down, kicking the dirt with his "first day of school" sneakers. When he came into the garage, he lifted his head, looked at me and announced emphatically "I'm not going back." Sam, not a huge fan of school to begin with, was obviously upset and angry. I was taken aback by his words and felt a pang of disappointment.

All day I had been thinking about all three of our kids, Sally, in ninth grade, and Berit in seventh, and hoping that they would come home enthusiastic about the coming year. I had imagined all of us sitting around the dinner table celebrating good news together. I said, "I'm so sorry" and asked, "What happened and who's your teacher"? When he said "Miss Prowley", my heart sank and I understood.

My first and only encounter with Miss Prowley (not her actual name) had been the previous spring at an outdoor band concert that was being held at the Middle School in West Boylston MA. My friend and I were sitting just behind Miss Prowley's sixth grade class and I spent most of the concert distracted by her interactions with her students. A sneeze by a student, a giggle, a look in the wrong direction, a whisper to a neighbor set her off and she would correct with a nasty look and a shake of her finger that said, "Wait till we get back in the classroom". What an unpleasant person, I had thought at the time. How safe and open to learning could a student possibly feel under her guidance? Thank heavens she is not one of my children's teachers, I had thought as I left the concert.

Miss Prowley had been a middle school teacher, not an elementary school teacher. What was she doing now teaching Sam's class? My whole body tensed with anger. Something had to be done. I told Sam we would talk more about this later, and to go play with his buddies for now.

Sam would love, I knew, to spend every day of his life playing in our big backyard and never ever again have to suffer the pain of school. The previous year, young as he was, he was already capable of some babysitting on our block. He was fun, gentle, playful, and creative, and was great at making up games or building forts out of pillows and blankets thrown over card tables or couches. He had a way and the kids loved him.

Sam looked like his dad when he was Sam's age, average build, a bit on the thin side, with a full crop of blondish hair. Both were passionate about sports to the point of obsession, so they had a great time tossing balls and watching televised sports. Sam was well coordinated and a very good athlete. He was shy with adults, didn't offer too much unless asked a question to which he would give you the shortest answer possible even if it was a "yes" or "no". But he was outgoing with his peers and well liked by the kids in the neighborhood. Like his two older sisters, he was easy going, inquisitive, and a fun companion, but like most kids had his moments when he lost his temper with me and probably sometimes for good reason.

Since I had never connected with any of my teachers, and school for me was an inconvenience, a nuisance to put up with, I felt empathy for Sam. I could hardly remember a time when I felt excited about learning. School left my mind clouded over with unpleasant memories, especially in the spring when I wanted to be outside.

Although spring is probably the hardest time to be in school for most kids with summer only weeks ahead, for me, the seemingly unattainable goal of succeeding by getting good grades as an indication that learning has taken place was so discouraging that it just increased my sense of not being smart enough. I just wanted school to be over. The accumulation of endless days of boredom with no excitement or joy made winter seem like it might go on forever. With the first days of spring I would begin counting the days till the last day of school and I could go to camp for the summer in New Hampshire.

The contrast between my experiences in school and at camp was so deep that even now I can vividly recall the overwhelming sense of aliveness, community, and freedom to learn in a totally different context that I felt there.

At home and in school, I was bored, withdrawn, and unhappy, but Camp Wabasso in Bradford, New Hampshire, was my childhood haven where the energetic child in me would come out of her cocoon, and express her aliveness and love for life. In the summer I came alive, swimming in Lake Blaisdell, playing tennis, riding horses, living in a community of kids my age and having crushes on the counselors.

Most of all I loved the feeling of community, living so connected with best friends in a cabin, sleeping, eating, and singing together. I never sang so much in my life as at camp. It didn't matter how good a voice I had. Every day, we sang, laughed, and sometimes cried together.

I loved the freedom I felt jumping or diving into that deep velvety dark blue water on a hot summer day from either the dock or the diving board. I loved the sensation of twisting and turning in the air, and trying different challenges like touching my toes before landing in the water, or pretending to be a swan by stretching my arms outward before landing in the water, or diving backwards or seeing how high I could jump in the air or how much of a splash I could make. I loved to learn different strokes: the crawl, the back stroke, the breast stroke. During our swim class time and during free swim my best friend Faith and I would make up underwater games like having teas parties or seeing who could stay under water the longest.

And although I was very shy and self conscious, I loved the nights when our counselor would take us down to the dock and we would take off our clothes and jump into the water naked. At first we would giggle and hide beneath our towels until we got up the nerve to show our bodies not to just our friends but to the whole world. What a sensation I felt when I first jumped into the water and the first shivery feeling when the water touched all those parts of us that we learned we had to cover up behind those itchy bathing suits. What a freeing, wonderful feeling!

Going to camp was like going home, and every summer, shortly after school ended, the long awaited day would come when my parents drove me to Grand Central Station in New York City to meet other camp buddies and a chaperone, put us on a train and for a whole day make our way from the world of suburbia to the magical woodlands of New Hampshire. It felt like another country. The first summer I went I was nine.

At the end of August when camp was over I would be faced with another school year always hopeful that this one would be better. I had convinced myself that disliking school was normal.

So now I didn't want Sam to feel the way I had about school. He deserved, as I did, a teacher who loved children and made an effort to see the world through their eyes: a teacher with real caring and understanding and joy, who could see the joy and good in all students. I only sensed then what I know without doubt now: that the number-one priority for any teacher is to create a loving, safe environment for children to learn in. Learning is a natural impulse. All children are curious by nature and the teacher's job is to keep that curiosity alive.

Unfortunately, Sam hadn't had a great start in his experience with school. His kindergarten teacher was loud and controlling, more interested in a quiet classroom than what went on in the heart and minds and souls of these vulnerable first-time school students. She got good behavior standing the child in the corner and shaming them.

It was his second grade teacher who sensed Sam's fear around school. She was responsible for making it a safe place for him for the first time. She paid attention to him and drew him out of his shell.

But now here he was, confronted with Miss Prowley. Watching him play with his pals, I realized I had my work cut out for me. In the school's eyes our job as parents was to toughen him up and get him to understand that the world is not always a "get along" place. We should, they would tell me, teach him how to deal with the Miss Prowleys of the world.

I knew as a woman and parent my chances of having an opinion heard and respected would be slight. And what did I know as a parent? Was I really going to take his refusal to go to school seriously, and let him get away without going to school? I could feel my stomach tensing and my body go into fight mode.

When Sam refused to go back to school the next day, I called the principal and we set up an appointment to meet together with Miss Prowley. In this setting she seemed responsive and pleasant, which left me curious, but skeptical. So I sought more information. Another teacher at the school lived in our neighborhood, and from her I learned that Miss Prowley was actually a frequent topic of conversation and concern among her colleagues, even if just based on her overall demeanor and not anything documented by direct observation of her class.

So when I asked Sam for more details, he told me, for instance, that she didn't refer to the kids by their name but by assigned numbers. She disciplined by making them stand in front of the chalk board with their fingers where the erasers rested. For some small kids, this was a difficult height. Also, on their way to the gym she made them all march in perfect lines and put their feet down on the stairs at the same time. If they got out of step, they had to start over again.

This was not the Miss Prowley who had come to the meetings, nor the one who came to a follow up meeting which included Sam as well as the school counselor. After that meeting, he told me that in the meeting he had barely recognized her. "Mom, she is not like that in our room," he said.

No decisions were made immediately, but the final opinion from the school was what I had actually expected. Sam needed to continue and to adjust. The overreaction was mine. I was being overprotective. I became the problem, not Miss Prowley. I felt I was being told that I was "only" a mother, and that all I knew was from my own experience, and that my feelings, intuitions, instincts were not enough.

All of this fed into a self-doubt which plagued me wherever I went. So I did receive some satisfaction when, two years and sixty children later, I read in the local paper that there was going to be a public school board hearing to hear parents' and teachers' concerns about Miss Prowley as a teacher. The outcome was that she was terminated soon thereafter. I also heard that she had been diagnosed with some form of mental disability.

Sam had been trying to communicate this message to everyone as well as a nine year old could.

Through all this and subsequently, I frequently found myself fighting depression, and didn't understand why. I had a wonderful husband and three healthy, normal children. But everything I had been told from the time I was a little girl about being totally fulfilled as a mother and housewife, was not what I was experiencing. Feeling unfulfilled as a wife and mother was not only shameful but indicative that there must be something wrong with me. The thought never occurred to me that something inside of me was trying to burst forth, trying to grow, expand. I was always the problem.

It was also at this time that I did read *The Feminine Mystique,* and realized that Betty Friedan was writing about me. She called my depression as a "problem without a name." I hadn't realized until then that my aspiration to be a housewife and mother was not just a result of my mother's example, but also the result of the media. Writers and editors of women's magazines in the 30's and 40's had targeted energetic career women. In the 30's and 40's, women's magazines had been publishing serious articles about the world outside the home such as, "Can the US have Peace After this War?" by Walter Lippmann, or "Stalin at Midnight" by Harold Stassen. When WWII was over, the content of women's magazines became limited to articles about women as housewives. By the time of my college years in the 1950's, though, only articles about women as housewives were published in these same magazines.

I was especially struck by Friedan's citation of this from Adlai Stevenson's graduation address to Smith College graduates in 1955:

> Once immersed in the very pressing and particular problems of domesticity many women feel frustrated and far apart from the great issues and stirring debate for which their education has given them understanding and relish. Once they wrote poetry. Now it's the laundry list. Once they discussed art and philosophy until late in the night. Now they are tired they fall asleep as soon as the dishes are finished. There is, often a sense of contraction, of closing

horizons and lost opportunities. They had hoped to play their part in the crises of the age. But what they do is wash the diapers.

The point is that whether we talk of Africa, Islam, or Asia, women have "never had it so good" as you. In short, far from the vocation of marriage and motherhood leading you away from the great issues of our day, it brings you back to their very center and places upon you an infinitely deeper and more intimate responsibility than that borne by the majority of those who hit the headlines and make the news and live in such a turmoil of great issues that they end by being totally unable to distinguish which issues are really great.

This assignment for you as wives and mothers, you can do in the living room with a baby in your lap or in the kitchen with a can opener in your hand. If you're clever maybe you can even practice your saving arts on that unsuspecting man while he's watching TV. I think there is much you can do about our crisis in the humble role of housewife. I could wish you no better vocation than that.

I was beginning to understand what was underneath my depression. I went to see a therapist for the first time in my life, but the results were unhelpful. He was a product of his times. Betty Friedan and feminism were radical for him. I continued my reading about these new ideas, and gradually change began to occur.

Though I didn't know it at the time, Sam's difficulty at school would play a part in my future transformation and fulfillment. We had been unable to resolve the problem for Sam and his school, so we enrolled him in a nearby private school. But eventually I would begin my own home school for him.

PART TWO:

TRANSITION - COMING INTO THE LIGHT - FINDING MYSELF

Chapter One

MEETING JIM NORTON

It seemed like such an insignificant event, that spring evening later in the year when Bruce called me from his office asking if it would be okay to invite to dinner a prospective new colleague, Jim Norton. "Of course," I said. "Should we be fancy or serve family style, as usual? " "He's very informal," Bruce assured me.

Before I tell of this event, here's a little background.

Bruce was the founder and director of an internship program for students called Dynamy, in its second year. It was perhaps the first so-called "gap year" program. While he had been teaching English for nine years at The Hill School in Pennsylvania, he was concerned to see that students seemed to lack life experiences to write about in their weekly journals. They were bright, but underexposed to life.

At the same time, having been representing the school in a multi-school study of the emerging educational needs of adolescents, he was becoming more and more intrigued with many writers like John Holt, Jonathan Kozol, Edgar Friedenberg, Kenneth Keniston, and John Dewey. These were psychologists, sociologists, and academics who were considered progressive thinkers writing about educational needs of young people.

For example, Edgar Friedenberg in his book *Coming of Age in America*, published in 1965, was writing about the experience of going to high school: its impact on the lives of high school students and on their later political outlooks. Theoretically, Friedenberg said, high school is intended to prepare its students to be citizens in a democratic society but in practice it trains them in submission to arbitrary authority. High school students have no inalienable rights; they have privileges granted to them in exchange for submission and conformity and taken away without reason or recourse. The degree to which this is so varies from school to school. Students from upper-class families have more resources for resistance. For this very reason, teachers dislike the idea of having to deal with such students. Many teachers like having their small measure of authority and resent any student who weighed it lightly.

Another example was John Holt's *"How Children Fail"*, first published in 1964, expounding on his belief that children love to learn, but hate to be taught. His experiences in the classroom as a teacher and researcher brought him to the conclusion that all children are intelligent. They become unintelligent because they are accustomed by teachers and schools to strive only for teacher approval and for the "right" answers, and to forget all else. In this system children see no value in thinking and discovery, but see it only in playing the game of school.

Besides these writers, he was also finding out about other new forms of experiential, student-center learning like urban semester programs, Outward Bound, independent study programs, experimental colleges like Simons Rock Early College, Hampshire College, and other new ways of approaching learning for late adolescents.

This was the first time we had heard the term "experiential education." In the late 1960's, it was becoming more and more apparent that, outside of the traditional models, students had few opportunities to explore decisions about their future and what they wanted to be when they grew up.

Dynamy was one of the first internship programs in the country created specifically to address that issue. High school graduates, instead of going on to their freshman year in college, took a year off to attend Dynamy, where they would do several working internships to try on different professions. They then would be able to enter college with more knowledge and self growth.

Bruce and his staff paved the way for Dynamy interns to immerse themselves in a year -long series of several internships by securing and networking a complete range of internship opportunities: various size businesses, organizations, labor unions, artisans and tradespeople, agencies, and government, with its base in Worcester, Massachusetts. The sponsors included everything from lawyers and doctors: to contractors and social agencies; from veterinarians and museums to weather bureaus, schools, and radio stations; from elected and other public officials to schools, banks, and large corporations.

Dynamy was also a community living, group seminars and outdoor challenge experience. Interns lived in group houses or apartments. Each house had an advisor whose job it was to not only help them to find internships but to help them communicate to each other their thoughts and feelings when conflicts or differences arose in their living environments. They learned how to operate as a family instead of independently. They had to discover first hand that they were part of a whole and that what they did or didn't do affected others. They had house meetings to discuss food, shopping, quiet hours, basic rules that made living together a cooperative adventure.

Jim Norton was interviewing for such an advisor position at Dynamy for the coming year.

So early in the evening Bruce arrived with our dinner guest. Dressed very informally, we shook hands and greeted each other with the usual polite "hi" and "how are you?" But during the course of the dinner, Jim began asking me questions, questions nobody had ever asked me before in my life. Not just: "How are you?", "How long have you lived here?", "What's your favorite baseball team?", "Where did you go to college?", "Where did you grow up?", "Did you have a nice holiday?"

These questions were different. "So how do you like to spend your time?" "What do you like to do the most?" "Tell me about your family? " "How do you feel about Dynamy?" "From your perspective is there anything you would like to see change?" "What's hard about being a mom?" "What are your kids like?" I was intrigued, more with my answers than with the actual questions.

I began sharing feelings, insights, and at one point, I could feel the tears coming as the answers to his questions seemed to reach deeper and deeper within me. Where was this coming from? I had never been here with myself in this way before. No one had ever asked me such personal questions.

At some point in the dinner, I had to leave and pick up Berit at skating practice. I found myself not wanting to leave for fear I would miss something. I didn't know what was happening but I knew something different was happening.

On the way to picking up Berit, my mind opened into a torrent of questions, including questions about questions: What was my fascination with Jim's questions? What had I really learned about questions, asking questions, both early on and in my lifetime? Was there some point where certain questions were too rude, too invasive, none of my business, especially if they raised feelings? And if you raised feelings in another, wouldn't you risk actually hurting them? How important are questions in order to know how you feel and think which seems necessary in knowing oneself? What had I learned about asking questions growing up?

And I thought of the questions I might have wanted to hear in my family if they had been curious and encouraging, as I had just experienced from Jim. What was the best part of your day in school and what was the most difficult? If you had a hundred dollars how would you spend it? What kind of music do you like and why? What color would you like us to paint the living room? What would you like to do to have fun? What it was like to hear about the war? How it made me feel? What do you think about President Roosevelt's death (or your cousin's death or anyone's death for that matter)?

Only much later was I to think of questions I would have liked to ask them, if I had had the voice and encouragement: Did you ever think of asking me important questions? Did you wonder about how I felt about situations but were afraid to ask for fear you might have to deal with my feelings, and maybe yours as well? Did you somehow believe that my stories didn't matter? And if so, did I matter?

When I returned Jim needed to leave, and there was no space for continuing the conversation, but what had intrigued me about meeting him was the connection I felt with him. His questions led me to feel not only curious about myself but also cared for by someone else. Someone else was spontaneously curious and interested in me. A window opened up to the questions I need to ask in order to understand others, and ultimately myself.

Chapter Two

RE-EVALUATION COUNSELING

One day soon after that dinner with Jim, our oldest daughter Sally came home for a long weekend from the Meeting School in New Hampshire, a small Quaker boarding school whose "campus" was a farm located in southern New Hampshire.

The years before Sally went to the Meeting School, she had attended West Boylston Junior and Senior High School. Time and time again she would come home from school upset and complaining about her French teacher. "She's mean, she yells at everyone and I'm not learning any French. I'm never sure if I'm going to be next on her list," she would tell me.

So I had gone to the principal and shared my concern about her learning French especially since she was eager to learn the language. I suggested that Bruce and I hire a tutor at our expense and that the tutor could administer the school tests as needed and Sally could get her language credit. Instead, without consulting me, the principal arranged that she would be tutored in French by a senior during the same period she would have been in class. The solution rescued her from her class, but she still didn't learn any French.

Sally had also begun to take a much greater interest in her education and had heard about The Meeting School through a friend. She was becoming very independent in many ways, wanting less and less of my input on anything. Since Bruce was such an entrepreneur in education and an excellent teacher and less involved with her on a daily basis, there was a developing bond between them now around her education. He was a great support for her coming into her own and finding her way outside the family into the larger world. So, on her initiative along with the help of her dad, she did the groundwork of looking into her options for schools and selected The Meeting School.

This choice seemed sound. We felt reassured watching her thrive there. From that experience she was to take charge of her life.

It was on one of her weekend trips home that I noticed a pamphlet about something called Re-evaluation Counseling lying on the hall table. After reading the first page I became intrigued. It was talking about emotions and how crying is a natural recovery process following a physical or emotional hurt. The book went on to talk about our social conditioning against emotional expression carried by our cultures and rigidly inflicted upon us when we were children ("Don't cry," "Be a big boy," and so on). By preventing us from expressing our feelings, this has interfered with, and prevented, recovery from our hurts, leading to an increasing accumulation of distresses and tension. By the time we are adults, this accumulation of hurts has severely limited our potential to achieve a sense of who we are in our essence and to enjoy our full potential as human beings. You can think of it this way: that our minds shut down and our thoughts get trapped inside the hurt.

At last, someone was giving voice to the emotional void I'm living in.

What I read went on to note that children are hurt when their inherent nature of needing to feel important, loveable, and valuable, does not get validated. The hurt carries the message of not being important, not being adequate, not being loveable, not mattering and then building beliefs around the hurt messages.

Further, children accept those beliefs as facts and create their lives around those facts because no adult has understood how impactful the message of love is, that it is more than putting three meals on the table but deliberate spoken words of appreciation and validation, and actions and expressions of love. An emotional language and vocabulary is critical to the developing self esteem and self love of any child. Self love is essential to the child's ability to love and value others as well.

I quickly made the connection to my own experience. Once those self limiting belief patterns such as "I'm not important", "I don't matter", "I have no value" or "I'm inadequate and unlovable as a daughter and student" began to shape my life beginning in childhood then I had concluded from a young age that I could not be anything other than a wife and mother. I couldn't even begin to conceptualize my being smart, even being smart in the culturally limited parameters of my growing up. That is, I couldn't even be a secretary, nurse, or teacher.

For the first time in my life now I was hearing that there was the possibility that these thoughts, such as "I can't think" or "I'm stupid" were not fact. How could I have been expected to learn anything when those were the prevailing thoughts wrapped up in the emotions that controlled my life?

With this new perspective and the tools the pamphlet described, I could learn to transform my beliefs about me by seeing how in my childhood my thinking had been skewed by those childhood messages delivered by maybe a grade on a paper or a grade on a report card or the seeming lack of interest taken in my education or my difficulty in reading comprehension. Maybe I'm not stupid. What a concept! There is nothing wrong with my brain. I was not born this way.

I had grown used to hearing people say some are born smart and some are born not so smart. So we all have our positive qualities and smart just doesn't happen to be yours, Betsy. Even saying out loud the words "I am smart" brought up a host of feelings. It was such a contradiction. But in order to accept the truth of being a smart woman, I would need to move through a host of feelings.

I devoured the entire book immediately! Soon afterward, I joined a beginners' class in Re-evaluation Counseling in Boston. The teacher was a wonderful, soft, gentle, articulate woman in her early thirties. In our first class she began by introducing herself. She was telling us a story about her young son who had come down with the flu and how the night before he had run a very high fever and how scared she felt. And right there in the class she began to cry. I was dumbfounded. I was embarrassed for her, I thought she was losing it; I felt myself losing my respect for her. I thought she was strong and now I saw this weakness in her. I couldn't believe it. Then she stopped crying. She seemed to have complete control over her tears. What's going on here? I asked myself. Then she began to talk about crying. She told us she could probably imagine what we were all thinking when she was crying. And she listed everything I was thinking. My god, maybe what I'm thinking is what everyone else is thinking.

She went on to talk about feelings and emotions and how we live in an emotionally illiterate society. I had never heard that expression before. She noted that we have been cut off from our feelings and the expression of them from the time we were small children. As children we were often told not to feel what we were feeling. If I had felt sad on a sunny day, someone might say, "You don't really feel sad. Look at how beautiful it is outside." I didn't want my children to feel sad either on a beautiful sunny day so instead of asking them to share what they were feeling, I would remind them of what a beautiful day it was and that they didn't need to be sad. Now I was hearing that you can't rationalize feelings. They are what they are.

My teacher was saying just the opposite of what I had known or learned. She was saying that crying was a healing process. It's a positive. There does not need to be any fixing, just loving caring attention, just someone to witness your pain and understand. The crying will come to an end and when it does that will be an indication that the hurt has been reevaluated in the brain, put into context and therefore healed.

I couldn't then imagine crying in front of anyone else in that class. I would feel humiliated and shamed showing my tears. So it did make sense I would feel this way: when I had felt like crying in my family I would quickly retreat to my room or someplace where no one would see me crying since no one in my family ever cried in front of anyone. I never saw my father cry and, in fact, I have no recollection of seeing my sisters cry. My father told the family that when he died he wanted us to have a party instead of a funeral. The goal was to be happy at all times. Now I could see that in fact there's nothing wrong with wanting to be happy, yet that pretending to be happy when you're not was the problem.

Even at the death of my mother's mother, to whom my mother was devoted and whom she took care of most of her life, and who even lived with us for as long as I can remember, I never saw my mother cry. At the funeral, she sat in another room and listened to the service through a loudspeaker. Only her sister sat with her. Not even my father or us, her children. At the time that had seemed to make sense to me because I had then carried the belief that you do not cry in public, period, not even in the presence of your family. After all, crying was shameful and weak. So now I was exhilarated to be learning a new way of responding to my emotions, though it didn't come easily to me.

About three classes later, I did cry in front of the class. I felt the tears come and instead of pushing them away, I let them come. It was one of the most liberating and courageous experiences I had ever had. It felt like a natural extension of that dinner with Jim Norton, where I discovered others could be interested in who I was and what I thought about things. Here I am, crying, and no one is freaking out. They are just giving me attention.

After a while, the fear of what others might think about me was gone and I could move more freely to express myself in the class. I could share some of the beliefs I held about me and the discouragement and pain I felt about my limitations, as if the feelings were fact. I could share my frustration of being a mother, wife and woman. I no longer felt like the outcast or the "sensitive" one in the family. Not only did I learn to reclaim my emotions by expressing them but to begin to widen my world view of who I was and my potential as a woman. My negative thoughts about me were being challenged.

How different my life would have been if I hadn't believed that my father's lack of emotional understanding and involvement meant I was a disappointment to him or that I didn't matter to him! If instead I had understood that what he was able to give me was all he knew. Or that not being a good student in school was not about my not being smart but about the lack of understanding and training my teachers had in addressing the way I learned. They also, no fault of theirs, lacked understanding of the value of looking for and pointing out students' positive traits.

As part of the class, we each chose a partner as our co-counselor and every week between classes, our homework assignment was to meet with our partner and listen to each other share whatever s/he wanted to share for an hour and then switch roles. Counseling meant giving each other warm and loving attention so that our partner could say and express whatever they wanted to during their time. I spent many a session with my partner crying and feeling my anger for the first time. I had no idea where it would lead me but I felt stronger and ready for change.

Over time, Bruce joined in participating in Re-evaluation Counseling and both of us attended many weekend workshops and eventually taught weekly classes out of our home. Now as I felt growing comfort and safety in expressing my feelings, my world and my mind began to open up. I participated in workshop weekends as often as possible, because I was hungry to grow and develop in the ways the approach fostered.

Chapter Three

EMPOWERMENT

One Re-evaluation Counseling workshop in particular served as another stepping stone in my path toward freedom and self-expression. It was an all women's workshop in Connecticut, addressing women and power. On Saturday afternoon, the leader of the workshop, a woman I'll call Susan, asked me if I would like to work with her as a client in front of the larger group of about thirty women. I was nervous, but I knew that working with her along with the energy of a group of women was a great opportunity to grow and deepen my understanding of the roots of my powerlessness. Maybe I'd be able to move through some of my powerlessness. This was the essence of the weekend.

I don't believe until then that I had ever understood what it meant to have power as a woman, or what was even meant by the word power. My mother had been my example of being powerful. In spite of my father having been the head of the house, she made the decisions within the household about raising the children, hiring and firing the help, food shopping, making sure my father's suits got pressed, his shirts ironed, and all his other needs met. She was the CEO. But outside the home, she was nothing. She had no power.

Now I was seeing that feeling important and mattering are necessary components of being powerful. If I could have previously defined my role as a leader, it would have been in terms of my mother's model. In this model Bruce's work was far more important than mine. He was the one who mattered. He was the smartest and the smartest ones made the money. Men like my father worked out there in the BIG world where all the leaders lived and exerted their power. That is where the power lived and in my experience, power was defined by the male world. Men were the leaders of everything important and the program handed to me was to follow them, not lead them.

And here I was, in the middle of the women's movement and at a workshop aimed at helping me understand what lay underneath those old definitions of myself. I was about to reclaim a part of myself that I had never known.

Now the tenets of Re-evaluation Counseling were teaching me that I came into this world with all that it takes to be a powerful woman. I was born with the capabilities to be powerful, to be in control of my mind, my actions, my thoughts, but in my growing up I had adapted away from all those possibilities in order to survive. I now had the opportunity to retrieve that power.

So there I was, standing in front of this group of thirty or so women all giving me their total attention. Susan held my hand and instructed me to look out at the group of women sitting in front of me.

"Betsy, she said, "Take your time looking at each one of them. Look into their eyes."

Because I felt so safe and secure with her guidance, I could already feel my tears begin to surface. I could see the love and concern and encouragement in their eyes. We were all here at this workshop, far beyond the fear of judgment of what other people were thinking about our crying and whether crying was good or bad or healthy or not.

I proceeded to follow the instructions of my coach. She encouraged me to continue to feel all my feelings knowing that a major part of this work involved opening myself up to my vulnerabilities. I let the tears come as I began to contradict all the negative messages with the positive ones. She asked me, "Betsy, I want you to model for the other women what a leader with a fine mind would look like." Just hearing her announce me as a leader contradicted a huge part of my beliefs.

She then instructed me to say to them, "I want you to look at me and see a woman who has a great deal of life experience and knowledge to share with you."

I could hear my voice getting softer and trying to shut me down. I thought to myself, "I'm too old to do this. And "I'm not smart." I could feel my crying build in intensity as these two contradictory voices came together. As the crying got louder, I began to feel freer and my voice began to sound more authentic.

Susan gave me the words to contradict the internal voices. "I will never again invalidate myself because of any lack of information I think I have or because of my age or anything else lest I mislead you into thinking that lacking information or getting older is shameful. "

Susan continued by encouraging me to work at this commitment, repeating it over and over again and paying attention to the tone of my voice, my posture, and the expression on my face. I didn't believe the words yet. I looked out at the eager faces, and in a firm, angry, confident determined voice which felt now like my inner intuitive voice speaking, I repeated the direction: "And that is a promise: I promise you," I told the women with an emphasis on "promise", "I will never again apologize or invalidate myself again lest I mislead you."

The hardest part for me to accept was the part about being smart. My coach assured me that that was a belief left over from my childhood and that the truth about me was that I held power and knowledge and that I was capable of learning anything I wanted to learn. She looked at me and asked the question, "Who has power and knowledge?" And I said in my loud forceful voice "I do." Now I was feeling shivery and sweaty and I felt the power behind my tears as if they were pushing against a wall that was beginning to collapse. Susan, in her gentle yet affirming voice, kept pushing me on. I could feel myself letting go of something big as my voice kept getting louder and stronger and my crying felt more like rage than grief.

I thought of the times I had given up with school principals and teachers before I had insisted they hear me. But behind the rage, I could also begin to feel empathy and compassion arising within me and that the behavior of principals and teachers towards me was more about their feelings of powerlessness to change the system than it was about me. They were not acting from a place of power. If they had been they would have listened to me and validated my thinking even if they didn't agree with it or act on it. Powerful people listen. How many times had I heard disempowered people say, "You can't change the system. You have to learn to live with it."

Now my confidence was really building and I started to say whatever came out of my mouth not stopping to analyze my words and hold back if I thought that others wouldn't agree. The tears were less victim-like and tougher, stronger. I continued to address the women.

"No more sympathy for each other. We have far more capabilities than we're putting to use now. We no longer have to worry about our reputations or what we look like, whether our makeup is on straight or our bodies fit the image of the perfect female or our clothes are the right color or fit. We are fine the way we are." Hallelujah!

I kept looking at the group and their attention was riveted on me. This time I began to address the mothers in the group.

"Because we are the main caretakers, no matter how much patience it takes we made a commitment to our children when they were born, to stand by them no matter how important other things seemed to us. We can do it no matter how difficult it gets. We can do it because we feel the power of our love for them." I realized how disempowered my father had been and how hurtful it was to him and Bruce and all men to have been taught not express their feelings. Finally I understood why my father had acted so disconnected from his role as father and as a part of the household.

And I felt so in touch with my love for Sally, Berit and Sam and wondered if I had been showing that love. And then I heard myself say, "It's not women's work. It's human work, and if we stepped out of our role of mother and housewife, which are simply labels someone put on us, we'd start acting like the powerful human beings we are and were born to be." By this time I had my old belief of "I'm not smart, I'm not smart enough, I'm not smart enough" surrounded.

I felt freer than I had ever felt in my life. What a powerful experience. But it was still only the beginning of my expanded horizon.

Chapter Four

THE HOBBIT

"If you don't like the way the world is going, then you change it. You have an obligation to change it" - Marion Wright Edelman

We had moved in 1973 from our three bedroom home in West Boylston with lots of yard and space to play into our six bedroom home in the city of Worcester, with very little property to play in, but greater convenience to everything else. I really thought the move would solve all my problems, different schools, children having greater access to activities in the city without relying on me to carpool them. At last I would be content.

After withdrawing Sam from public school and Miss Prowley, we had transferred Sam to a private school nearby, for his third, fourth, and fifth grades. Though he was certainly in an improved and safer learning environment, we had concerns about both his academic progress and also a confusing inconsistency in staff competence and style. Was the difference worth the private school tuition we were paying?

So by early 1974, not seeing any school options that would both reflect my own emerging beliefs about learning and also be responsive to what I saw as nurturing and supporting Sam's growth, I began to think about starting my own school in our home. Though secondary, I also thought that if we were to be spending money on his education, why not create my own program - for certainly no greater expense? And I had heard of home schooling, although I didn't know anyone who was actually doing it.

When I mentioned my idea to Bruce, he cheered me on. So the following fall, I began a home school, which I called The Hobbit, with six students including Sam. They were all neighbors so they could walk to our house. The first year I enrolled three girls and three boys between the ages of ten and thirteen. The second year I enrolled four girls and four boys. (In describing students in the chapter, except for Sam and his best friend Chris, their names have been changed).

Our family lived in a large, but not fancy house. The entrance to our main school space was through a side door of the house which led to a short set of stairs going down to a semi-finished basement room, which became our common room and where we gathered the beginning of each day. I covered the rough cement basement floor with end carpet pieces, hung pictures on the wall and found a fairly decent couch and some chairs for sitting. There was also a ping pong table off in a corner.

On the first floor I created a small library room off the front center hallway. There were two large windows, one opening to the porch in the front of the house and the other facing out to the side of the house. The room was empty of any furniture. Instead, the floor was covered with a plush bright Kelly green carpet which was covered with large bright colored pillows. We called it our library because one whole wall consisted of built-in bookcases. We often met in that room because it was warm and we could sprawl out on the floor. The living room across from the library also served as break out space when students needed some alone time or talking times with a friend. On the same floor at the end of the hallway was a kitchen and large dining room with doors that led out to a side porch... So there was plenty of space to operate a small home school.

In the fall of our first year, we began The Hobbit by going on a five-day fall camping trip to New Hampshire. Bruce's Dynamy always began its year in the fall with a three and one-half week Outward Bound experience in the White Mountains. The purpose of the Outward Bound experience, according to Kurt Hahn, its founder, was to help young people develop confidence, independence, and teamwork through the rigorous outdoor experience of living – in our case hiking through the mountains, sleeping under tarps, and cooking, in all kinds of weather. He believed that this kind of program helped young people "overcome the misery of their own unimportance," and that in developing teamwork, you understand how much you and everyone matters in helping one another stay alive and safe. It also helped students in the three and one-half weeks of outdoor living and hiking to get in shape and adapt away from the culture. So doing a mini-Outward Bound with my crew seemed appropriate for the same reasons: to develop confidence, teamwork and an understanding that the choices we make affect the outcome.

I hired an experienced Outward Bound instructor, Marty, to help me lead the hikes, teach such skills as making a fire, and in general teach the kids about living in the wilderness, issues of safety, and a sense of respect and connection with the environment.

We spent the first week of school preparing for the trip, finding tents and setting them up in the backyard making sure all the poles were there as well as other essentials in putting up tents. To arrive to our campsite and find out we were missing a pole would be a catastrophe in my book, so I wanted to be especially sure we had everything. We settled on two tents, one very large and the other medium-sized: boys in one, girls in the other. Together we created a menu and then did the shopping together. We planned chores, who would be in charge of cooking and who would be responsible for cleaning up. We made lists of what clothes to bring and what clothes not to bring. After all the bases were covered we took off for New Hampshire along with our Hobbit mascot, our very large five year old golden retriever, Luke.

At daybreak on our first morning I was surprised at how frustrated I felt watching Ted and Chris organize the breakfast. I was so used to doing everything myself that it was a challenge for me to watch someone else take over. Breakfast was cold cereal, milk, juice, and fruit, but finding which of the many coolers or boxes the food was packed in required endless opening and closing and digging, and searching, and uncovering. I could hear Chris yell out "Betsy, which box is the cereal in" or "Where are the spoons and bowls?", and, "I can't find the milk", which made me realize I could have done a better job of labeling. I continued to resist taking over and eventually everything showed up on the table. And we all ate. Cleaning up was even more of a hassle since hot water was not there on demand; it was necessary to go to the stream and cart the water back, turn on the stove, and heat the water in pans. Washing cereal bowls, zipping up tents, safely putting the food away in containers, all took longer than I had expected. My patience received a good workout.

What seemed like hours later, we were off to climb Mt. Carrigain, at 4,680', one of the highest peaks along the southeastern ridge bordering the Pemigewasset Wilderness area. I hadn't climbed a mountain for twenty years. I became so busy making sure that each of the kids was organized and had the right gear, including rain gear and water bottles and first aid stuff, that in the end I forgot my raincoat.

When we reached the trail head, Marty set the ground rules. The main rule was that we hike together as a group the whole time and that we walk the pace of the slowest walker, which in this case was Karen. She was the youngest in the group and the smallest but with plenty of energy. Even though she was the slowest climber and took many rest stops, for which I was grateful for everyone, this was a great accomplishment for her. This was her first attempt at climbing a mountain. The older kids like Patsy and Ted and Julie were very patient and even though they wanted to hike at a faster pace, willingly followed the plan.

Ted had the most experience in climbing and hiking. He was somewhat of a loner in the group but a gentle soul and full of curiosity and information. His parents had recently moved to Worcester. Prior to that Ted had been attending Quaker schools. I'm not sure how they heard about my school but since there were no Quaker schools in the area, they liked the experiential part of my program. Patsy was the oldest and tallest of the group, very athletic, confident, bright, and cooperative. Julie was a year younger than Patsy and Ted, but the most enthusiastic of the whole crew. She exuded cooperation! She was so happy and grateful to be in a program like the Hobbit that included climbing mountains as an important educational experience. Chris was ten and this was his first mountain climb. Although he complained that his shoulders were killing him from carrying his daypack, he was a good sport and kept going in spite of the problem. Chris and Sam were like brothers. Chris's parents had been concerned about his disinterest in school and the fact that he didn't like to read. The reading "problem" didn't seem to improve so they thought an experiential program would stimulate his interest. He was of small build, with a crop of curly brown hair. He was sensitive, curious, cooperative, and very athletic. Since Sam had only sisters, having a buddy down the street became monumental. Many a night Chris spent with us and many a night Sam spent at Chris's house. They both loved sports, following the weather, playing practical jokes on the phone, and enjoyed just being together. Sam had a more difficult time waiting for the group but he was willing to control his pace, and I felt proud of him.

We all made the five mile hike up and down Mt. Carrigain without incident, tired but in good humor. In spite of strong winds at the top of the mountain, when we took our last step off the trail surrounded by scrub bushes and into the open panorama at the very top, the view of the surrounding mountains took our breath away. I felt as if I was standing on top of the world. While at Camp Wabasso as a camper, I had always felt a sense of accomplishment when I reached the top of Mt. Kearsarge, elevation 2937 ft. Since Mt. Carrigain was nearly 2,000 ft. higher, I felt that same feeling at this moment. The kids were ecstatic and running all over exploring each crevice and overhang.

Going down the mountain was easy in comparison and we arrived back to camp by late afternoon. After unloading the gear from the car on return, the kids were sent off to find a special place within sight of the tents to do some writing in their journals, which I explained would be a daily practice here as well as when we were home. In the front of the journals, they were to write about what they had done today and in the back of their journals they were to write about how they were feeling today. The feeling part was a bit of a challenge, namely to separate out thoughts and feelings, but we would be talking more about that as the year progressed. I wanted them to at least begin to understand the language of feelings. I told the kids that night as we sat around the campfire, "When I act grouchy and short with you, I notice how little patience I have, and that I am feeling tired. I will tell you, when I hear myself snap at you or raise my voice, that my impatience is not about you, but about my feeling tired. I tell you that so maybe you will write about your feelings the same way."

By the middle of this trip, we were all sleeping together in one tent. The boys' tent was a disaster area, so we had decided to all sleep together in the one large tent. Being together felt cozy and warmer.

The last night there, Ted had found a stranded mouse in the campground men's room, which he brought back to the campsite. Karen became the designated caretaker of the mouse. Everyone rallied around this poor little pathetic motherless mouse. Karen tried to make a home for it in the top of a Clue game box, but of course everyone wanted to hold the poor creature so he went from being held underneath a warm winter jacket back to the Clue box lid. That night he slept in Karen's sleeping bag and by morning he was dead. During the night Karen had rolled over on top of him and that was the end. That morning we had a burial.

But with all of us in the tent together on that cold previous night, I felt a moment of such bliss. As I had looked around at the group, each in their sleeping bag and writing or reading, I had felt a sense of peace, as if the whole world was in this tent right now. This was the moment that counted, because I was feeling a connection to each one of them. The experience of the last few days, living outside and watching them take charge and work with each other had been a great beginning. What a great way to start off the year!

Once back in Worcester, we began the program I had developed, one influenced largely by my own experience as a child, a parent and a student of Re-evaluation Counseling. It was important to me to de-emphasize the classroom as the only setting for learning and expand their experience into community resources like the Worcester Art Museum and other museums, the public library, City Hall, the courthouse, and historical places where major events had taken place. Expanding the classroom to include the whole city made sense to me as a way to develop in the students a sense of belonging, responsibility and pride in their city and environment. My goal was to shift school spirit to community spirit.

So the city became their classroom. We toured every historical site in the Boston area from Plimoth Plantation to North Bridge in Concord to Louisa May Alcott House in Concord to the Lexington Historical Museum to the Willard Clock Museum in Grafton to the Salem Witch Museum and many others. We spent two mornings a week in the Worcester Public Library where the library staff taught them how to use the card catalogue system, the microfilms, pamphlet files, and periodicals. They also created a library scavenger hunt so as to help them put their knowledge to work.

Over the period of eight weeks, they were introduced to the Worcester Art Museum collection. Two of the students became junior docents. The students also became familiar with the justice system by attending a murder trial where the defendant was acquitted. They witnessed the selection of the jury and many questions were raised about the defendant and Judge being black and the jury all white.

They interviewed a candidate for the state legislature, a writer, a city councilwoman, a state legislator, an environmentalist, the city mayor, and even Jonathan Kozol, the author and educator, when he was in town to address students at Holy Cross College. I had called him and told him about my program and asked if he would to come visit our school before his lecture at Holy Cross and let the children interview him. He came and spent about forty-five minutes with the kids asking them questions and letting them ask him questions.

I organized two scavenger hunts a year which involved using the public transit system. In pairs, they had to locate various sites inside and outside the city by taking a bus to a particular destination and home again. I wanted them to be self sufficient in getting around and feeling safe in the process. They loved doing this. Two of the girls reported back that while they were walking down Main Street on their way back to school, they were stopped by an older women who in a sharp voice asked why they weren't in school. One of the girls replied by asking her why she wasn't at work!

We also toured Old Sturbridge Village and on one of a series of visits the kids dressed in nineteenth century clothes, each one spending the morning either as a museum apprentice working with the cooper, or the cabinet maker, or at the Freeman Farm helping with chores, or at the Fitch House learning to spin yarn.

The students continued to keep their daily journals, recording what they did each day and how they felt about what they were doing. This continued to teach them the importance of feelings and how to name the feelings they were experiencing.

Since I was not a teacher, I saw myself as more a facilitator for their learning. I hired Holy Cross students to come to the house two mornings a week to teach math. This was the only traditional subject that was taught, all of the others, like social studies, writing, reading, art, science, were learned experientially.

We began every morning together. Each shared what was new and good in their lives, setting goals for themselves, and learning to appreciate themselves and each other. I could see how easy this was for the girls and how difficult sharing feelings was for the boys. Already at their age, anything that required or implied intro-spection or feelings was a no-no, and finding a way to help them do this was a huge frustration for me. Even getting them to listen and not react was a challenge. The boys' way of avoiding their feelings was often to mimic the girls. I had a difficult time addressing this because my old emotions from childhood often got triggered. Every once in a while I would take one of the boys upstairs and give them a little talk about feelings, but to little avail. They had already been indoctrinated into the ways of being male in our cul-ture.

One morning in the winter time I woke up feeling discouraged, not sure of myself. Maybe the feeling of "not enough" was creeping into my thoughts. I was dreading hearing that back side door open in just an hour or so and hearing those little feet go clunkety-clun-kety down the steps into our school room. Negative thoughts were gathering in my brain like bees swarming around their hive. I decided I needed to take a risk in our morning meeting and to share with them what I was feeling and thinking. So feeling a bit appre-hensive, while getting dressed and eating breakfast, I wondered how to do this. Finally, I realized I had nothing to lose.

When everyone had arrived and morning meeting began, I told the kids that I was feeling discouraged and wondered if the things we were doing were helpful or interesting or even fun. I asked them to write about either their frustration or their appreciation of the school. I was expecting some moaning and groaning, but after scrambling into their packs for paper and pencils they began to write enthusiastically. I was surprised. I left the room while they wrote. When I returned, the notes were sitting there in a pile of let-ters, some of the most positive, appreciative notes I could have imagined. It was as if each them was waiting to be asked their opinion. Not only did I feel a renewed sense of purpose, but they felt that their insights mattered to me. It was a pivotal moment for me. My energy level went up 100%. .

Chapter Five

GROWING FRUSTRATIONS

As growthful and rewarding as creating The Hobbit was for me personally, and as predominantly positive as the feedback was from the kids and their parents, by the middle of the second year of 1975-76 I realized this was only a temporary solution for Sam's education as I saw it. His situation had been my prime motivator, and without this impetus The Hobbit would have never been created in the first place. And this program was essentially for middle schoolers like him. He would not be a middle schooler forever. Also, I was also becoming more and more aware of how limited my field of knowledge was and how frustrating that was to me at times.

Also by this time, much else had happened in the two years previous, for Bruce as well as for me, events and changes which were making some major family decisions necessary.

One particularly significant set of related events involved Berit and my experience with her school.

One day early in 1974, I had received a call from Berit's school reporting that she didn't feel well and asking that I pick her up. We had enrolled her the previous fall as a ninth grader in this private day school, which had an excellent academic reputation and was only ten minutes away. We had friends whose children attended there.

As I pulled the car up to the school she was sitting on the steps with her head resting on top of her books. This was the same spot I picked her up twice a week to take her to the figure skating lessons I noted earlier. Skating was the main love of her life and she skated at least four or five times a week. I loved to watch her small, athletic body move across the ice in one of many skating outfits I loved sewing for her. I felt a sense of pride every time I saw her spin or land a jump or skate backwards and with confidence turn direction. As I sat in the stands watching her skate, I wished I could do the same.

Her skating had begun back in the winter 1971-72, when we were still living in West Boylston. Bruce had built a 60'x40' foot enclosure in our backyard and flooded it to form a skating rink. He even created his own version of a Zamboni, which he used every night to make new ice for the next day. Although the neighborhood kids along with Sam played hockey on the rink most afternoons, Berit had also gotten her start there and soon after began taking figure skating lessons.

Watching the kids skate from the kitchen window, I also had felt the urge to want to skate also. After a few searches for the box where I had stored my skates when we had moved, I found it tucked away in the basement with other never-unpacked boxes. The skates fit perfectly. I felt excited and started skating, sometimes at night with the floodlights mounted on the house providing the necessary light on the rink or on some nights with just the full moon as my guide. Or I skated during the day when everyone was in school. I felt challenged going back and forth from one end of the rink to the other on one foot and holding my balance. I soon became intrigued with skating again and not long afterwards began skating lessons. I had found something that turned me on to life and who I was. Skating would thereafter often help to contradict my doubts and anxieties about my life, and also excite me about expressing my energy in fresh ways.

But this time picking her up was very different. As soon as she got into the car, she began to cry, saying she really wasn't sick but didn't know what was going on. She had been in her Latin class and all of a sudden she felt funny. What she was describing sounded to me like an anxiety attack. This reminded me in a way of my experience with Mr. Flynn's back in his seventh grade classroom. She had felt faint, her heart racing, so she had left her Latin class and gone to the nurse's room. I was imagining that as a first year student, she must have still been feeling nervous about being in a new environment, leaving old friends, making new friends.

When we arrived home, she seemed to be feeling a little better. I made some tea for both of us to sip on as we sat in the kitchen and talked about how school was for her and about her fears of making friends.

As we talked, I thought about the school setting up support groups for new students, a place where they could come and ask questions or share experiences, how they felt about being the new kids on the block, what they may need, what was helpful and what wasn't.

That afternoon I called the headmaster and asked if I could come in and talk with him about my idea. I should not have been surprised by his answer which was a polite assertion that they already had the support resources needed, one of whom was the school psychologist.

Here we go again, I thought to myself. Regardless of how well-intentioned the headmaster, I took a clear message in my mind: "You know nothing. Get back to pouring the coffee and baking the brownies and helping to drive the kids to their field trips." Basically I was in the way. By then I had experienced through Re-evaluation Counseling over a year of rich excitement learning about emotions, communication and listening, but in many ways this new knowledge and excitement made my life even more frustrating, because even armed with the new knowledge and perspective I had lacked in my earlier dealing with Sam's school and Miss Prowley, still a person in authority didn't want to hear about them. Again, when I wanted to step in and be part of an education team I was politely denied.

So, as with Sam's earlier case with Miss Prowley, at the end of that school year we enrolled Berit in another school, also private, which as an all-girls' school offered what for us seemed a better social environment and sense of empathic community, reasonably solid academics, and more flexibility in program. Unlike the change for Sam, however, for Berit the change to the new school was, if not ideal, at least far more than adequate and well worth the relatively modest tuition.

Chapter Six

WE NEED CHANGE

During this time Bruce had also been experiencing more and more dissatisfaction with his work at Dynamy and with his relationship with himself and his role. He had in the first years of his job felt enormous satisfaction with meeting the challenges of starting a new venture from scratch, and of seeing the program solidly in place and thriving. But now he had scaled down his responsibilities, and arrangements had been made to end his assignment there by the middle of 1976. He was now in many ways also uncertain where he wanted to head with his own life and thus ready to think outside the box.

So with this ingredient, combined with my ending role as home schooler for Sam, and my own interest in expressing my creative energy, in whatever form that might take, we decided we had to make a drastic life change. It suddenly felt almost imperative that to do so we make a clean break from our roles and routines: we decided on a self-styled sabbatical to put into perspective all that we had both been assimilating from the last four years and see where they might take us. The Re-evaluation Counseling we had been doing had pointed up the self-contradictions in our lives, the dichotomies between our beliefs and our actual life, but had not resolved them. Time was needed to measure careers and commitments. We were ripe for the very thing Bruce had created for young people in Dynamy: a program of our own to test our information, our emerging ideas and values against reality in a new frame of reference. We had no idea what that time off would lead to. After much conversation, we finally decided to take a full year to see what would emerge.

So it was that by early 1976, we identified and began to implement what we had named our Vision Quest Year. After many evenings talking about the year ahead, we had decided to spend the year traveling and exploring the United States and to buy a trailer in which we would live for a year. We had hoped that traveling and seeing different parts of our country would help to stimulate our thinking and open perhaps a whole new path.

Was this even possible? Many signs pointed to yes.

Berit was about to complete her junior year in high school. With support from her school and agreement to receive credit for the experience, she had decided to enter a program called the Trailside Country School for her last year. Through the program, she would journey around the entire country with about twenty other students and four staff, studying and interacting firsthand with many different natural and cultural environments. The program drew on a wide collection of local resources including just plain folk all around the country. The students worked as farmhands with Mennonite farmers, caught cod and squid from a lobster boat in Nova Scotia, climbed several mountains and learned about the environment from local naturalists, forest rangers and college professors. They lived with the Hopi Indians conducting oral history interviews. They slept outside every night in the desert, in the mountains, in the Grand Canyon, on the ocean beaches in the Virgin Islands. They lived out of a large yellow school bus equipped with a built in library in the rear of the bus, and built in storage space for equipment and food and a huge rack on top of the bus where backpacks were stored. I'm not surprised that her interest in science and the environment later became a focus in college, and then in life.

After graduating from the Meeting School in 1974, Sally had postponed college in favor of working locally. She was planning to take at least one more year off before college so as to know more about what she wanted. She had already made plans to live with a family, helping out with childcare and writing her autobiography.

As for Sam, who was thirteen, he would of course be coming with us. Although he acted amenable to a whole new adventure, in retrospect, what choice did he have? Saying good-bye to his Babe Ruth League baseball team and all his friends, especially Chris, was not easy. Chris's mother had confided in me that this was also really tough for Chris who was not only losing Sam but also losing The Hobbit. That was the hardest part about leaving for me also. Chris and Sam were like brothers, and Bruce and I had grown to love his company.

So everyone's needs in our family would be addressed during this sabbatical year for us. In a sense, we were all about to head off on our own individual sabbaticals.

What about our finances and giving up any paid income for at least a year? We had lived well enough on our salary, but we had never saved or invested or put away anything for retirement, let alone something like this. Nor did we have any outside help or independent income. We had only some equity in our house and some inherited stocks and our possessions.

By careful calculation, we projected that by selling our house, stock, and most of our belongings we could generate enough cash to buy portable transportation – a trailer - and live modestly for at least one year or possibly two. At worst, we thought we could always abandon our plan if circumstances demanded it, and return to work. We were, after all, still both in our early forties. We also reasoned it was not great security we would sacrifice – we were already living at considerable risk by all standards of conventional middle-class prudence. So when it came to financing college for the children, that would likely require financial aid, loans and working their own way.

And what about all our possessions? I had in the first years of our marriage bought into the articles in the women's magazines implying that the more possessions I had, the happier I would be. We had everything anyone could want and still there was part of me that was caught up in having even more. The larger our house, the more things I believed I needed. In becoming more and more disillusioned with my life as it was evolving, I had for years dealt with those feelings by buying more and more things: a new lamp, new curtains, more kitchen gadgets, or appliances, a table or chair; and also to spending more on home improvement: painting, remodeling the bathrooms, or buying new carpet. Scaling down all these belongings in order to move into a twenty-five foot trailer presented challenges, but for me this challenge was irresistible: by then I had realized that maintaining a well cared for house and its furnishings were what actually kept us from being adventurous in the first place.

So I was ready to give up the house, most of our possessions, and all the chores and required maintenance (including the small vegetable garden, which was mainly Bruce's), good neighbors, a quiet tree-lined street, and easy access to shopping. Our house sold fairly quickly. Soon afterward we held an enormous yard sale and got rid of most of our belongings.

I felt a weight lift off of me. It was difficult to envision telling my mom that we had sold many pieces of furniture she had given me, but I wanted to explain to her that it gave us an opportunity to buy challenging, life-giving experiences out of which would come our inner growth, our real security something that builds within and goes wherever we go and cannot be taken away. But I never did tell her. She would never have understood, so I didn't bother.

Typically, the rest of my family said little about our decision although I'm quite sure much was spoken amongst family members. I had no idea what they were thinking, but had learned to accept their silences.

In July we bought a 25' Airstream trailer and realized right away the challenge we had to live in such minimal amount of space with our fourteen year old son. But we found ways to take what was important to us. Our downhill skis hung from the ceiling. Every item had a special place. Organization was of the utmost importance in order for us to survive in every way. When we travelled our bikes were stored inside the trailer. The dining room table collapsed into our bed at night. Sam had his own bed toward the rear of the trailer separating his space from ours by a sliding partition. He also had a small television to keep him up to date with the world of sports and weather, his two loves. The kitchen fit somewhere in between with a two-burner stove, a small oven, a small fridge, and a surprising amount of storage space. The bathroom was in the very rear and even had a shower. It also converted into a darkroom with space also for my photography equipment. Our 1970 Ford LTD Country Squire station wagon had been outfitted to pull the trailer.

By summer's end, and with most of our belongings having been sold and the house vacated, we found ourselves saying goodbye to neighbors and friends. All that remained was to point our rig down a highway. We knew certainly that ties to where we were coming from – both material and personal – had now been dramatically severed.

Chapter Seven

ON THE ROAD

At last we were on the road, feeling free and excited about the unknown, what tomorrow would bring. I remember vividly that moment of departure – feeling alone and nose to nose with the unknown, and yet excited. Our only home was our trailer and various places to park it: a borrowed driveway, a campground, or a parking lot.

We found our bikes to be a great source of fun, exercise and convenience. We rode them all around Washington DC from the Washington monument to Mount Vernon along the Potomac bike paths. We pedaled twenty-five miles through the Gettysburg battleground. We rode through the fertile landscapes of the Amish country in Pennsylvania in the pouring rain. Late in the fall we watched the sugar cane being cut as we bicycled through the Cajun country in southern Louisiana. We played golf on public golf courses wherever we could find them, played tennis on public courts in small towns throughout the south and southwest. We spent preelection days in New Orleans where Jimmy Carter only days before he was elected president addressed a Mardi Gras-style rally in Jackson Square in the French Quarter. We took a ride down the Mississippi River on an old river steamboat. We experienced our first cold weather in Big Bend National Park in Texas when the temperature went down to 26 degrees and the desert was covered in ice. We heard the coyotes at night and saw deer on the mountain roads. We followed the Rio Grande River through the Boquillas Canyon. We spent subsequent months crisscrossing the southwest and then back to the southeast. The trip was a truly varied firsthand cultural and geographical education.

As the months wore on through the winter, though, we often found ourselves confronted with what lay ahead in our future. We wondered how long it would take for new ideas to surface. We found ourselves in intense personal discussions addressing what we thought were our strengths? Our interests? Our skills? Our needs? Our priorities? Our goals? Our commitments? And, beyond the continued fresh experiences of each day, were we actually any closer to any decisions?

 In between, also, there were brief reunions with old friends scattered around the country in New York, Virginia, Louisiana, and Texas. We hunkered down at many campsites and palavered with other vagabonds.

As for keeping Sam up with school subjects, there was daily writing and math with his dad as his teacher. There was a continuing learning curve concerning trailer and vehicle maintenance. And we did lots of reading about current issues especially those of global concern, the environment, the population, food supplies, nutrition, sexism, racism, other oppressions, and the world economy. When we were traveling, Sam sat in the passenger seat next to his dad, connecting with him in conversation and/or reading to him the latest sports biography he was reading, or talking about their beloved Boston sports teams. Bruce was, in so many ways, the dad I didn't have. Although he was, like so many men, emotionally distant, he was totally invested and connected in the lives of his children. Even on this trip, he shared his love of literature and poetry in so many ways.

"The Silver Bullet" – 1976-77

PART THREE:

The Butterfly Emerges

Chapter One

The Decision to Begin a School

Part of our trip took us later in the winter to Minnesota and the Twin Cities. Visiting with an old friend and Dynamy colleague, we learned about a summer job possibility at a large boys' camp in Northern Minnesota, Camp Lincoln. The camp directors were looking for leaders, preferably a couple, to be the directors of their intermediate division. The camp was located on Lake Hubert in the heart of the lake region. The long waterfront reached from one end of the camp to the other and the possibilities for swimming, sailing, boating, plus other activities like horseback riding and tennis were endless. The job sounded great for us as well as an excellent summer opportunity for Sam to be with his peers and to participate in a full range of sports activities. We accepted the job when it was offered.

This job turned out to be one of our most fun summers in a long time. The experience brought back for Bruce and me fond memories of how much we had loved camp when younger, especially the close feeling of community engendered by living in cabins, eating in the dining hall, singing round a camp fire on a very starry night, and all in all living with the vibrant energy of young people. The staffs of counselors, mostly from the Midwest, were talented and dedicated; their sense of humor and unsophisticated way of inter-acting with the kids and with us was refreshing. They played as hard as the campers. Many were teachers in the winter and camp counselors in the summer.

We were also able to put to good use all of our recent life experi-ence and our newly acquired information, awareness and perspec-tive about young people and education and learning, in particular their need for self love and self esteem. As we came to appreciate the deep impact of this experience on the campers, in how it com-bined learning with fun, the environment, a sense of community, and a sense of relevance to life.

Thus, our thoughts kept pointing us back toward working in edu-cation, the vehicle through which we believed change was most possible and for which we had the passion and interest. We found ourselves brainstorming with other staff members and counselors and found a number of our camp colleagues quite curious, ener-getic, and even available to follow us where we might be headed.

And it became clear that if we wished to have the best qualities of summer camp as a partial basis for something new, we would def-initely be looking at something that only partially resembled what comprised a typical school. We would be creating something very new. Thus was planted the seeds for beginning what was to be called Baker River School ("BRS").

Chapter Two

BAKER RIVER SCHOOL
BECOMES A REALITY

When we returned back east from Minnesota at the end of the summer, and with no real place to call home, but joined by several of our camp cohorts, we decided to look in the New Hampshire area for a piece of rental property as a base of operations, not necessarily the site for the school. New England was a favorite place of ours, especially New Hampshire. Bruce had graduated from Dartmouth, and of course New Hampshire was where I had spent so many wonderful summers at camp. By stroke of luck and word of mouth from friends, we located a large piece of rental property which was also for sale on Ellsworth Hill in the Baker River Valley town of Wentworth, New Hampshire. The property looked not only like a temporary base of operations, but possibly even the site for the school. Up until that time, we had been looking at the possibility of pursuing an original plan formulated while still at Camp Lincoln, namely finding an existing summer camp and developing the facilities: winterizing the cabins and adapting other buildings for school needs. Since New Hampshire had an abundance of camps, that had been our focus until we discovered the future Baker River School on Ellsworth Hill.

Once we committed our intention to begin a new school, everything went into planning our first moves. In November of 1977 Sam would turn fifteen. I actually don't remember sitting down and having a full conversation with him about his thoughts and reactions to this idea and what his options would be, whether he would like to go to this new school we were creating or to a regular high school. For him, this situation may also have been reminiscent to him of the start of The Hobbit, where he didn't have a choice either. I didn't know what he was thinking - just making some assumptions he would think this decision was a great idea. Maybe I had already concluded that in certain situations like this young people depended on their parents to know what was best. So this decision was basically not his.

In all of this, I was as much the child as anyone else. I was still trying to find my voice, maybe at the expense of neglecting my role as a parent. Because in reality, did he really have an option? If he had said public school, once we had found our location in Wentworth would we have really been willing to drive him every day back and forth to the closest high school twenty miles away in Plymouth? Or did he realize that he had no choice but to go along with the program, so why fight the system? I'm guessing it was probably the latter. Perhaps the issue of peer friends was far more important than school itself.

Periodically the old voices in my head drowned out the new innovative voice I was claiming. Maybe he needed to go to regular school like all other fifteen year old teenagers and do the same old thing that teens have been doing forever. Maybe we were crazy to think we could pull this off and have this building built, recruit students and staff, and develop the whole program by the following September and the opening of school. And maybe my mother was right to worry that her grandson might never have the opportunity to go to college. Fear, fear, fear. Maybe we were actually ruining his life. My deepest fears, which I never shared with anyone lest they would think I was crazy (and that maybe I was!), was that if he went to regular school, his life would continue to be consumed in sports and the weather, and, after all, wouldn't most parents want their kid's lives to be consumed with sports? Wouldn't that be a healthy thing?

But I really wanted more for him than high school had to offer him. No one could take his love of sports away from him. Love of sports was built into his genes. He would always find a way to play baseball, skate and throw a basketball into any hoop in the neighborhood. But what about the rest of him, that gentle nurturing side and the creative side of him. Would that part of him be able to survive high school? Would he learn or even have the time to like music or appreciate the world of art or be given the opportunity to climb mountains and explore the wilderness as part of his educational experience? Would he have to live the rest of his life like most males in our culture as my father and to some extent Bruce had done, living in this emotional void and perpetual definition of what it means to be a "real" man in our culture? Real men do not have feelings. I thought life experiences outside of the classroom should continue beyond The Hobbit and be a part of his high school education as well.

We had our moments of fear but somewhere inside of both of us we believed that what we were doing was good, healthy and extremely important. My passion for change, for giving a language to our feelings, for life bigger than the Red Sox or the world of sports or the weather seemed to outweigh everything else. We were making decisions that would affect him the rest of his life.

So we moved into the large six bedroom yellow farmhouse at a crest near the top of Ellsworth Hill. We rented at first. We were at first simply excited to find a place to plant our feet, especially after a year of living out of our trailer and not having a home base. Having our own bedroom, even with only a mattress on the floor, seemed like a luxury in itself. But within a short time, when we saw that no other option seemed workable and saw the obvious fit between this property and what we envisioned, we began work on actually purchasing it.

The property included 112 acres of land comprised of a wondrous variety of woods, streams, and fields. The fields just above the farmhouse were thick with blueberries and wild flowers in the summer. The fields outlining the woods would be perfect for playing frisbee, cross country skiing and general all round outdoor recreation. The woods were abundant with sugar maples for a possible sugaring operation, and with ash and beech for firewood for our wood stoves, which were our main source of heat. A clear water pond, about an acre in size, would be accessible for winter skating and summer swimming.

To the existing house and barn we would later add The Dorm (built 1978), The Greenhouse (built 1981), and Moose House (purchased from a neighbor (1981).

I remember standing on the front porch of the farm house, a late 19th century colonial structure later to be officially dubbed the Yellow House, on a mid-October afternoon on one of our first days there in that fall of 1977. Looking out at the spectrum of orange, yellow, brown, red, and gold leaves forming a frame around the sun reflected on Mt. Carr in the middle distance to the east, I could only imagine how many women in the past had stood on this same spot on a similar beautiful fall day watching this same mountain fade into darkness. I could only imagine what dreams, and hopes they had carried for their lives on top of Ellsworth Hill. They were farmers' wives, cooks, mothers, grandmothers, and widows, their stories unknown, untold. Hearing their struggles, comprehending their strengths, and hurts could have inspired and connected me in a deeper way to the land, the climate and life on Ellsworth Hill, but like so many women they were invisible in history and their stories were never told.

Later, after the opening of BRS, my relationship with Ellsworth Hill Road became one of love and hate. The most intense frustration came especially in the winter, in particular after a snowstorm. The whole distance was quite steep, but halfway between the bottom of the hill and the top there was a section of especially steep incline, where vehicles without chains or four-wheel drive would start sliding and skidding and end up in the ditch. Again and again, Bruce had to be summoned by yet another frustrated driver to come down with a hand winch (a "comealong") in our old truck. There was always the challenge of dealing with the unique positions of these vehicles and creating a tailored strategy for extrication. This happened enough times that eventually we decided in the winter-time and during the mud season in the spring to park all our school vehicles at the bottom of the hill, except for the truck with the plow, which remained at the top for emergencies. Even after giving classes to everyone on how to put on chains, we decided that it would be better all way round for us not to bring the cars up hill. Everyone would simply have to walk the steep mile to and from our cars.

The road was public, maintained by the town (population 375) as much as the town's limited resources and the road's poor drainage patterns allowed, but because the road basically ended at BRS except for an unmaintained extension to a few summer weekend residences behind our property, it was in effect mostly our private road, convenient and ideal for running, sledding, meditative walks and overall use. Also, in the spring Bruce tapped the sugar maples which lined the side of the road and filled the nearby woods, boil-ing the sap down to provide the school as much as 30 gallons of syrup one season.

Yet when we first moved in to the property, little did I know that within a few years I would be walking the road in every season of the year and at any time of day or night with the serenity and con-fidence matching that of any of the night time creatures. It became my source of fitness, recreation and kinship with the woods. Many a dark cloudy night I walked that hill alone with no moon to guide me. There were familiar landmarks along the way such as an abandoned sugar house and a seasonal cabin about halfway up. As I would near the top of the road and just as there seemed no end in sight, the road turned just slightly and there in the distance were the lights of the yellow house. What a warm, inviting sight! Each time I walked in the night, I felt that sense of relief as well as accomplishment. Home at last and safe.

All of this was of course to come. But during the first weeks we were there, I can remember Bruce splitting and cutting firewood by hand in his special spot just down from the barn to the west. I can still see the sawhorse and the pile of wood, collected from what had been left behind in the fields and woods by loggers and past occupants. Bruce spent a good part of each day methodically cutting the logs up into stove length pieces, one after another after another. He reported that he could feel his arms get stronger.

We also immediately realized that we needed tools and other supplies and equipment, items, be they household or food, which were not readily available to us. We were learning about the limitation of our dirt road and reminded that we didn't have the luxury of being able to get what we needed right away, with the closest main town Plymouth nearly 20 miles away. We discovered that running over to the mall or the supermarket to pick up a needed item was a luxury and we would have to learn to keep lists of things that were needed so that when someone went into town, which might only be once or twice a week, we were very systematically organized and didn't omit anything.

The road in so many ways was a reminder that we were a community separate from the village of Wentworth and although dependent on the village in some ways, we were our own self sufficient community at the top of the hill and the road is what divided and connected us.

So there was a great deal of excitement we both felt coming here. We were going to start something from scratch. And we felt scared and apprehensive as the future was filled with unknowns, and questions yet to be answered.

Road's end: the Yellow House

Chapter Three

OUR EVOLVING GOALS

Meanwhile, while everything else was going on, we were meeting frequently to discuss our goals and design our curriculum to meet those goals. We centered on two questions. First of all, if education is an ongoing process of preparation for life, that is to say, for what is to come, then what does life, in the broadest and most fundamental sense, require young people to have information about in order to live a full and rewarding life? And second, once this first question has been answered, how then can a school –our school— best make it possible for our students to get that needed information?

These were not new questions for Bruce and me. We had been developing clear ideas about education and its responsibility for the human/emotional side of students for nearly ten years dating to Bruce's study while at The Hill School and extending to the Hobbit and Dynamy and Re-evaluation Counseling, concepts which were shaping our planning and discussion sessions. But these ideas did need further discussion, consensus, and fleshing out, not just between the two of us, but among the several other former staff at Camp Lincoln who had joined us in New Hampshire on a volunteer basis and whose support as well as thinking was essential, especially since this experience was for them very much a trial run with no firm commitment to join us as of yet.

So it was here in the Yellow House that we developed via consensus several principles that would guide our decision making, all of them resting on the concept of the school as a community. We wanted to create a community that embraced the domain of emotions, the language of feelings and how feelings get enmeshed with beliefs systems that become confused with our reality and keep us stuck in our learning and interaction with the rest of the world.

To accomplish this, we concluded we wanted to teach the tools of Re-evaluation Counseling and push students to think outside the box that contained their limiting childhood beliefs. As I had dramatically learned in my workshop experiences such as the one described earlier, when I was being counseled in front of the group, thinking outside the box does indeed bring up the anxiety and fears, yet that does not mean that one has to continue to allow them to hold anyone hostage to the beliefs and fears of their past. When I decided to think of myself as free and smart, I could make choices that would move me through and beyond my fears of not being smart rather than making choices that kept me stuck in the negative feelings and limited my life.

And so we committed to showing our students safe ways to release the negative feelings without unconsciously acting them out in a negative way either on themselves or others. We wanted, too, to give students opportunities and permission to connect with their stories so they could discover the source of their hurt feelings from the past and how those unprocessed hurts impacted everyday decisions in their lives.

We also wanted to create a community of listeners who could not only see and appreciate and validate the good in others but also in themselves. By sharing and expressing our love we could reinforce our own essence.

We also wanted to create a community where the kitchen was the center of the community and everyone learned about food, where food comes from, how to prepare various recipes, understand the chemistry of food, and how vital food is to our survival and aliveness and ability to feel in the first place. For me, it was wanting everything I never learned about growing up.

Further we wanted the young people to be able to develop a strong compassion for the earth and understood our dependence on it for our survival.

We wanted to create a community that thrived on having fun and bringing music into their lives.

We also wanted to create a community where experiential learning was as important as book learning. We brainstormed ideas, which later were to come to fruition in such events as trips to Washington DC and the state capitol and legislature in Concord, joining in Quaker weekend work camps in Philadelphia, participating in rallies of a political nature, such as the Women's Pentagon Action in Washington DC in 1981, joining demonstrations against completing the Seabrook Nuclear Power Plant, following as it was the near-disaster at the Three Mile Island nuclear plant in Pennsylvania.

We wanted to create a school that taught that all questions were good; no judgments were to be about them. Learning how to go about posing the best questions, and then learning how to go about getting answers would be what mattered.

And finally, we wanted to create a community that included, appreciated, and supported the parents and their efforts to be open and receptive to change as well as forming the backbone of the school community.

This would be the school of my dreams!

In order to realize these goals, we developed the concept of dividing the school year calendar into five modules, the first two in the fall and before Christmas, and the last three between January and the end of the school year. Each module would have a special theme with an emphasis on individual and group projects. Besides regular year-long courses in math, history, English, and lab science, the school year was divided into these modules:

> Well-Being- study of our connection to our most immediate environment which is our bodies. Subjects included sexuality, food and nutrition, first aid, and drugs.

> Science/Environment – study of our connection to our environment, the natural world. Subjects included animal life, geology, ecosystems, population growth, economic geography and food supply.

> Communication/Creativity – self-expression through such media as music, writing, visual arts, and pottery. Also, conflict resolution and decision-making skills through peer groups, men's and women's groups, and community meetings, all to support the building of school community.

> History/Social Science – studying and connecting to contemporary world issues such as oppression, economics, racism, social classes, energy, nuclear energy, and energy in general; also seeing government in action firsthand through trips to Washington, DC, and Concord.

> Expeditions/Internships - seven -week expeditions to the Southwest and Southeast or individual internships away from the school.

Besides these pieces in the curriculum, what interested me most, though, was the community with its emphasis on the emotional side of learning, giving language to feelings, a language that didn't exist in my youth and had so deprived me of knowing who I was, applying everything I had learned from The Hobbit, Dynamy, and Re-evaluation Counseling to a school community.

Chapter Four

OUR ROLES DEFINED

If Bruce were writing his story here, I imagine he would be con-
centrating on the financial end of the school – finding and manag-
ing the money.   In preparation for his role as financial manager, he
taught himself bookkeeping that first summer.   He drew up and
managed the budget and was a relentless monitor of the money,
turning every one of our limited dollars to maximum advantage.
He paid the salaries, paid the bills, collected tuitions, made sure we
had the insurance that was needed, made sure we were properly
incorporated as a not-for-profit educational organization and oper-
ated in compliance with the state board of education, health and
safety standards requirements, and filing of reports. When the time
came for financing the actual purchase of the property in the middle of our first year, he also negotiated gifts and loans from friends
and prospective parents, and then found a bank that would give us
our mortgage.   All I know beyond that is that every month I, like
everyone else on the staff, would find a monthly pay check on my
desk for $300. That would amount to a total year's salary of $3600.

He also acted as general contractor with responsibility for timely,
within-budget completion of two major construction projects:
housing for students.

He was also responsible for the academic side of the school.   He
was the most experienced teacher on the staff, having earlier taught

high school English at every level for ten years. He developed the formal piece of the curriculum, and what courses should be taught for how much credit. He kept the records and assisted students in the college application process for those who intended to go directly to college after BRS.

This story, however, could also be told from the perspective of our relationship, how a project of this size affected us as a couple. In short, there was little or no time for our relationship. In fact, by our final year of operation, we were living in separate houses!

Our relationship wasn't bad. The issue seemed to be finding time to have one! I can remember missing him and some nights would go to the cabin just beyond the pond where he lived, my sleeping bag in hand, and climb into bed next to him and make love. We rarely sat together in morning meetings, because he would be playing the piano, one of his favorite pastimes, to accompany the singing. We ate together but always with other students. On occasion, we took a weekend off and went to a motel for a Saturday night.

In other words, time alone was rare. We didn't even have enough time to disagree although if we did the disagreement was because we were both trying to protect our turf. On one occasion, I made a suggestion to cancel classes because I had been introduced to a very interesting Native American woman who taught a unique style of basket weaving. She offered to come to school to teach her skills. I was impressed with her and her interest in our school and I thought her visit should take precedence over classes. Bruce thought classes were more important. I don't know how we worked this out but I believe that eventually we compromised and set up some evening classes to replace the morning classes.

As head of buildings and grounds, Bruce also managed our construction projects. To comply with code, there was a bracing but by no means impossible list of items requiring attention. For example, we needed a new springhouse for our water supply, which was nearly half a mile away from the farmhouse back up in the hills. Visiting friends pitched in to roll a new six hundred pound concrete well tile half a mile through the forest to its new home at our spring house, and then build a cover. We needed smoke detectors, an alarm system, and improved fire escapes. The State required that all exterior doors needed to be rehung so as to swing outward. Little did we know that certain outswinging doors were later to be the source of many memorable frustrations. Because our buildings were exposed to winds which blew with great regularity and speed, certain doors would when swinging out be caught by the wind and find their way to freedom from hinges and end up some distance out in a field, usually at some worst possible time in the middle of a winter storm. Each rehanging meant new strategies, though none ever succeeded fully.

Actually this door law never made sense to me when applied to our unique situation since during big snow storms, when snow accumulated, someone had to go out another way and shovel the snow from doors so they would open.

Betsy and Bruce in an infrequent moment of connection

Chapter Five

BUILDING THE DORM

So during the summer before the fall opening of Baker River School in 1978 we built a one story wood and passive solar-heated dormitory which would house 16 students. Within the next four years, we added two more buildings to the property: a small saltbox house we built to house six students and two staff, with a greenhouse attachment. Hence the name: The Greenhouse; and an existing small three room cottage on seven more acres of property, which we purchased from a departing neighbor who had actually lived there year-round. Our other four neighbors were seasonal. Their homes were not in actual view and were little-used, even in the summer.

"I'm going ut orm" ("up to the dorm"!), I remember two year old Molly saying. She was the daughter of Linda and Tom Curran, two staff members. They were an adventurous, resourceful, handy, and multi-talented young couple we had met at Camp Lincoln. They had been married just a few years and were looking for something new and exciting in their lives. They had actively participated and lived with us in every stage from the start, as we located the school property, moved in, and planned the curriculum and community first year. They were also a hands-on integral part of building the dorm as well as creating the curriculum. They were with us for two years.

Martin, a prospective student, (I have not except for Sam and Chris used real names here or elsewhere) and his dad came to visit the school the spring before the dorm had even been built. Martin's school was closing so they were looking around for a new school. We were standing outside the barn looking east up the hill behind the yellow house when Martin's dad asked me where the dorm was. I pointed east behind the yellow house to a piece of ground just below the blueberry field and said with the utmost confidence, "This is the location for the dorm and where the building will be standing come fall when we open the school." Where did all that confidence come from? I had no doubts at all, not the slightest hint of a doubt. It would be there.

That was May. In early July we broke ground for our ingenious one story 60 x 40' passive solar frame building with partial post and beam construction. Among the countless tasks, I remember the labor-intensive dismantling of an old stone wall across from the Yellow House. We would load the rocks by hand into our pickup and drive over to the foundation site not far away and dump them onto a large bed of foam board insulation so they could serve as a heat sink when the sun's ray were captured through a long panel of south-facing windows.

Also, pouring the concrete foundation provided a challenge. A major problem we ran into was getting the concrete up the hill. At the entrance to our road from the state highway, there was a stream crossed by a "six-ton" bridge, meaning it was not safe for heavier loads than six tons. The concrete truck making the delivery was too heavy to cross. So we had to press a local dump truck into emergency service to bring the concrete up several cubic yards at a time. It took at least six trips. Such one-of-a-kind measures were common in the two-month construction process as we continued this learn-by-doing experience.

As part of the passive solar principle, the entire south-facing wall was to consist of essentially triple-glazed full length windows, and the building was to be super-insulated from top to bottom. Also, two wood stoves were to provide all the backup heat we needed in colder weather and on overcast days. The building was also to have eight student rooms plus a small two room apartment in the rear (for us), plus two large bathrooms, and a 20' x 30' central common room on the south front.

Over the course of the next two months, we built the dorm in one of the most intense, creative, hardworking periods of my life. People from all over came to help us. Our usual helpers, including especially new staff member and construction chief Tom Snell and his family, plus assorted contacts who were perhaps there more out of sympathy than skill, and who would come for a day or two and pitch in. Other new staff members joined as they were hired and arrived. Sam and other incoming students also helped. We never knew who would show up but we were always eager and grateful when they did. We would feed them well and put them up for as many nights as they were willing to work. As for Tom, he was by far the most skilled and experienced builder, having built his own house. Both he and his wife Julie were also part of our new teaching staff for the next year.

What a commitment this was, as well as a challenge, and with no pay! Building the dorm was totally dependent on the good will and volunteerism of others. I am quite sure that without the skills and directions and commitment of Tom, the building would not have been built and the school would not have happened. When in all good faith and honesty, I had told Martin's dad that the building would be there in September at the opening of school, I really had no idea what building a building entailed. If I knew then what I knew later, I may not have felt quite as confident.

The dorm under construction

Sam on construction crew

The newly completed dorm in winter

Rear view of the dorm from the field above

Our family - first Christmas at BRS

Sam on the Yellow House Porch summer 1979

Chapter Six

HIRING THE STAFF

At the same time we were building a dormitory, creating a curriculum, recruiting students, and meeting state requirements to operate, we recruited a teaching staff.

Beyond obvious subject competence the staff needed to be in sync with our goals and willing to be pioneers, risk takers, in this new adventure, all at a very small salary. Over the five years, we recruited eighteen different staff members total. In any given year, we had from six to ten staff, including us. This was the most dedicated, committed group of teachers I've ever known.

In hiring, first of all we wanted the staff to be open to the language of emotions. They had to be willing to share themselves openly and authentically, which sometimes required that they put fears of losing face aside. We expected them to use their power only as a vehicle through which young people could build their own.

Because our program was unusual and as demanding of the staff as of the students, they needed to feel as passionate as we did about our goals and the need for change in education. One of those changes, for us, included giving young people the experience of an expedition into the wilderness for three or four days at the start of each year, with only their essential needs—food, sleeping bag, flashlight, cup, spoon, one shirt, one sweater, rain gear, all carried on their backs. As one staff member wrote one year about his goal for students embarking into the wilderness, it was "to introduce their hearts to the singing beat of our environment." I would add to that: to smell the smells of the trees, of wet leaves, and to walk in the wet soil when the sky suddenly darkens and the rain comes. And to give them a taste of their intimate connection to the earth and know directly that life depended on how we understand and embrace that connection. So our staff needed to be reliable and experienced back packers and outdoor leaders who could handle the fears and anxieties of those young people experiencing the wilderness for the first time. And of course, they had to feel deeply connected with the environment.

Bruce was insistent, and I agreed, that one requirement for all staff was that they be drug- and alcohol-free, not only at school but in their life outside as well. This meant not even a beer over winter break. It was important to us to prove that having a good time was not necessarily dependent on alcohol or drugs.

Bruce had given up alcohol about five years before, soon after his mother died. Until then, we had followed the rituals of many families, which included having a vodka and tonic before dinner. We had always done that. But after Bruce's mother died, he realized that alcohol left him depressed, so he stopped drinking. I had felt somewhat annoyed with him because I was left drinking alone. It was no longer something we did together.

When I had started The Hobbit, I decided to follow Bruce's good example before taking the students on our four day trip to the mountains. I actually found myself feeling more alert, energetic as a result and so had already given up alcohol completely.

Most important of all, we needed staff ready to develop skills that would unite us as a team when we disagreed or felt annoyed by each other. Students needed to experience the adults in this community as a team. Our teamwork would form the basis for a safe environment in which students and staff could learn and flourish and grow. Therefore, we needed a sound structure and process for listening to each other when we disagreed and for being open to our differences and model how to work through conflicts. If we could learn through our own experience how to do this, then we could teach and model this to our students.

Ever since my introduction to the principles of Re-evaluation Counseling, I had become more curious and passionate about what I had learned. As mentioned earlier, during the year before our vision quest, when we were still living in Worcester, I had taught out of our living room a series of classes in Re-evaluation Counseling. In those classes of eight or nine we were able to create for each other a safe environment in which to share our feelings and thoughts, without fear of someone trying to "fix" us. As a group we learned not only to share our vulnerable sides which came out of our histories but through sharing our appreciations of each other, we each felt a growing sense of self- love and respect which would move us into a very different place in our futures. We were rebuilding each other's foundational beliefs about ourselves through our positive insights about each other.

Bruce and I believed this spirit could and needed to be repeated with the new BRS staff. So another requirement for a prospective teacher was that s/he be open to learning the language of emotions through being in a staff group, learning together the tenets of Re-evaluation Counseling.

Our concept of a strong viable school community would manifest through the expression of appreciation for all that was good and positive in the students and staff. In my school experience and that of my children, the focus had always seemed to be more on what students had not done well, and on what they had to do better. We wanted the staff to encourage learning by paying attention to what each student achieved, no matter how small the teacher might judge that achievement to be. We were convinced that growth comes from building strengths and letting students know that their learning matters and that every question that they ask matters. The fact that the students knew this would be an incentive to stretch beyond what they believed was their potential. We and the staff would show them that and model that expectation.

Later even students who were asked to leave the community because they weren't able to hold to the rules or didn't attend class or couldn't be depended on for work crews or kitchen crew, would be sent off with a list of what we saw as their strengths and potential: what we liked about them, positive things they had done during the time they were at school. Although their contributions hadn't been enough to keep them in the community, at least someone had seen the good in them.

Chapter 7

BUILDING A COMMUNITY

September 17, 1978 was the opening day of school, a small community far away from the mainstream, consisting of 15 students and a staff of seven committed to learning and living in a community with:

- No TV
- No soda or junk food machines
- No drugs or alcohol
- No sugar
- No computers
- No neighbors
- No gymnasium
- No competitive sports

Students almost never failed to be confused by their first encounters with our fresh approach to community living, which led to new ways to express feelings, connect with the environment, and communicate with teachers and with each other. Granted, they usually knew a lot about us through the application process, a previous visit to the school, and prior associations with one or more member of the community. But it was still an abrupt change.

Of the 15 original opening-year students, it turned out that less than half were fully ready for our curriculum and our community – ready to learn and to contribute right away. This handful of students was, however, to be enough to give the school a nucleus that would hold during our dizzying and often "what-next?" first year, but not with much to spare. Some of the students ill-suited for Baker River School had come as an option to a bad home situation, a bad school situation, a bad peer relationship—or all of the above. Most, while not malicious or deliberately disruptive, were simply not ready to make a right turn in attention, behavior, and commitment. Frankly, we were not that selective about who came at the start. In a sense we couldn't afford to be. But all this remained for us to learn, and to learn from, during the year and years ahead.

Interestingly in 2004, 21 years after the school had closed, we received a long e-mail from one of the students we had had to let go. He had been at school for only a few months before we had to send him home. He couldn't meet any of his commitments. In his long e-mail he wrote that he had wanted for so long to tell us about his experience at BRS and what had been going on for him at home at the time. From the time he was very young, he wrote, he had suffered from sexual and physical abuse at first by a friend of his mother's and later by his stepfather and eventually by his social worker. Coming to BRS, he had carried the blame for all the abuse, telling himself he was at fault, that he wasn't enough, had no value, and was basically a nothing. So he had no respect for himself. By the time he came to us, he was more interested in taking than giving.

He now shared that while at BRS he had had great difficulty accepting any goodness or love directed towards him and, in fact, he felt angry when people expressed any caring for him. He didn't deserve it or believe that could be true. Not until two years later, after a short time at BRS, and now 18, when he hit rock bottom, did he begin the long journey of learning and recovery and realize some truths about himself. He had come to remember BRS and the messages he had received about his goodness and how he didn't have to have the right behavior in order to be loved. The fact that he couldn't meet the commitments required for good standing in the community didn't mean he didn't have value or worth as a human being. He remembered our morning meeting his last day at school, and how, before he had left, people were wishing him well and telling him what they liked about him and saw as his strengths. He wrote that the seed had been planted then in that last meeting and even though he didn't know it, the seed remained there. Later his strong faith in God changed his life, but he wanted to find us to tell us that no one had touched him so deeply in so little time as the message of BRS.

Since that e-mail, Ben has become an important part of our lives. He came to our BRS 2007 reunion and shared his story with everyone there. In a recent letter to us, he told us that every day he tries to apply the important message he received from our meetings in the common room. "I love you, I appreciate you, I am listening to you, and what you say matters." That is the essence of who he is today.

The students who did thrive during the first year, though, were motivated and ready to pitch in, more than able to meet all appointments, which included classes, work crews, and required community meetings. Some of them chose the school because they were not succeeding in their present environment and wanted an alternative.

Grades were not at the top of the list of criteria for admittance. What mattered was character, ability to get along with others, willingness to live outside of mainstream America, a spirit of adventure into new areas of learning and challenges like backpacking, and a readiness to participate in all aspects of the community from cooking to chopping wood to washing dishes, as well as tackling the academics of the school. In short, to own their share of the workload of what it takes to live in a community and make it work.

With each year, we attracted more and more students who chose to come to BRS because of its philosophy and program rather than it being the last option. Many we knew from either Worcester or through friends or recommendations from other students or parents.

For students life was not only suddenly different but also tough in the beginning, living a new routine and process for relating to teachers and to learning. Dealing with emotions was confusing and unsettling at first. Mostly, the only communities they had ever known were the homes they grew up in and the schools they had attended. And no two came with the same values or view of things, since every family has its own rules, language, traditions and rituals. Teachers in a parental role were very new for many of them and calling them by their first name was unheard of, maybe uncomfortable at first. They could often understand but still not know exactly what to do with the new information.

BRS life differed from what students had been accustomed to at home. Just take eating for instance. We made a conscious effort to serve locally grown, fresh, home prepared food. Fresh fruits and vegetables when available in season (sometimes from our own garden) were the center of our diet, along with lots of whole grains. There were no soft drink machines, no snack machines, and no ice cream machines, and no access to them. White sugar was not available. Coffee could be bought individually but not available at meals, nor was white bread; all bread was whole wheat and homemade. Very little processed food was served, and no precooked food. Except for popcorn sprinkled with brewer's yeast (that was a favorite), snacks were not available. We also didn't get the usual endless stimuli to the appetite through television and other advertising.

This caused double confusion to many students, who despite an interest in good nutrition, usually came from an "eat anything" environment. Even if their families were food conscious, parents couldn't protect their kids from the environment that surrounded them with junk food. This meant an often long, gradual and ago-nizing transition period for some. One student survived for many weeks on peanut butter and jelly sandwiches, before he gradually began to expand his list of edibles and experiment with such (for him) exotica as eggs, fresh vegetables, granola and fish. He even-tually even mastered tofu.

The double part of the confusion lay, however, in dealing with their friends back home. Caught between eating patterns or in the tran-sition between two patterns, many of the students were, at an intel-lectual level, convinced of the merits of the new diet they were seeing at BRS. Thus they would often find themselves trying to convince friends of the merits of tofu and in the process generate confusion in their friend's minds about what was happening up at this unusual place. But regardless of whether the issue got a pub-lic airing at home, it still existed in the minds of students. And it wasn't confined to diet.

Every possible piece of waste was recycled. All leftover food and biodegradables were composted or recycled. Water was carefully monitored for the benefit of septic system maintenance. Toilet flushing was limited to "if it's brown, flush it down; if it's yellow, let it mellow". Hot water was especially monitored. Paper products were used in limited amounts; paper plates or cups were used only on two or three special occasions each year where guests required them; otherwise we used our regular yellow vinyl plates. This con-cept was carried a little too far at times. On one of the rare occa-sions when my mother came to visit from New Jersey, she was not given a napkin, so she asked one of the students if he would get her one. The student came back with some toilet paper. Although we did have a supply of paper napkins, some students were known to go to the extreme to conserve. She laughed, but I have no idea what she was really thinking.

Heat was supplied by wood, cut from our own woodlot and worked up completely by community labor; what oil was used in our one furnace in the Yellow House was strictly monitored, with our one thermostat set at 58 degrees. The remedy for being cold was to put on more clothes or to get closer to the stove. If someone wanted something from the nearest store (four miles) they walked. Transportation was pooled, and visits to Plymouth (twenty miles distant) limited to van trips on weekends. Laundry was done by the most energy efficient means - a laundromat in town. Electricity use was also carefully monitored and any unneeded lights were immediately turned off. High energy use appliances were not used.

In the winter of 1979, in the midst of a huge snowstorm, about four in the afternoon we lost our electricity. Dusk was approaching. We had to make some decisions quickly. No electricity meant no water beside what was held in our outside underground holding tank, because without power the pump was inoperable. We had six oil lanterns which we immediately put to use. We placed three of them in the kitchen so that the dinner crew could find their way around. We provided candles on the tables in the dining room and the other three lanterns in the three common rooms of the student living areas.

We called a special community meeting to set guidelines and answer questions and reiterate that no candles be used in student rooms. The risk of fire was too great. We explained that the volunteer one-engine Wentworth fire department would have a very difficult time getting up this hill and disaster would certainly prevail. We asked that students use their flashlights. Students' rooms were very basic, especially in the Dorm. The dorm rooms were more like camp cabins than finished bedrooms. Each room in the dorm had two sleeping lofts and a couple of shelves per student for clothes. In order to give the rooms some personality students used their creativity in many different ways by draping colorful sheets over windows or creating wave like effects on the ceiling by tacking long strips of light material over the ceiling. The walls were covered with pictures and posters of favorite artists or musicians or favorite slogans. Each room became a work of art but also a fire hazard. The thought of candles in the rooms was very scary so we hoped we had gotten our fears across. Mostly we went to sleep early and woke up with the sun. With so little light, evenings gave way to sleep. The following three days were a very interesting time and made us all think about how much of our lives were driven by electricity.

Beyond these practical imperatives, the curriculum differed vastly from what students had experienced at home: projects were self-generated; students could always help set the content and the pace in any course; Student/teacher relationships were open and informal- the schedule could always be changed to meet an urgent need; information was presented in a way that tied it to a larger frame of reference; the morning news took the form of an in-depth commentary on a single topic each day. Asking meaningful questions was as important as the answers that might emerge.

And the entire community, from dress to policy setting procedures, also differed dramatically from what occurs in the mainstream of our society. People wore whatever they wished. There was no competition for stylistic appearance. There were no seduction games. Women wore hardly any makeup. Openness and non-sexual physical contact like hugging were encouraged. So were sharing feelings, giving everyone an equal opportunity to do so, having staff and students share and share alike in the process, having everyone get equal air time for sharing thinking as well, welcoming the ideas of everyone, setting policies by consensus, and having clearly agreed upon policies relative to drugs so that communication can be guaranteed .

Also, we were always seeking out root causes rather than being confused by symptoms in dealing with any issue (whether local or worldwide); cherishing cooperation rather than competition in our sports, games, and community activities (certainly a contradiction to traditional school systems); breaking down sex/age roles in work jobs and positions of responsibilities; speaking out.

All the above set a tone and a climate at distinct variance with what prevails to some extent everywhere.

By its very existence, we suppose BRS in many ways, especially in our community meetings, showed students that ideals in communication could be implemented and that sometimes, the hard times in the community led to a deepening of understanding for each of us and how through our actions or inactions our behaviors fed into the strength or weaknesses of the entire community. Conflict really served as an opportunity for growth: here we didn't need to be afraid of our differences or our stories. Regardless of our stories, everyone mattered, and everyone made a difference. Our goal was to build an emotionally aware community.

Chapter Eight

COMMUNITY MEETING

Note: All names except Bruce's and mine have been changed in this chapter.

Community meetings were a vital part of life at Baker River School and could be called by anyone who wanted to bring up an issue that she or he thought was important to the community. The meetings gave everyone the opportunity and permission to tell their stories and to share their feelings and thoughts in a safe environment with the intention of strengthening our community, calling attention to policy issues, and addressing conflict.

Infraction of the drug policy was by far the hardest issue to deal with in our community because drug use in so many cases served to cover up larger problems not as easily addressed. I'm not sure how fully drug free our community was at all times over the years, but I know each year we gained more ground. We considered the infraction of the school drug policy a community issue, and therefore had to be dealt with by the whole community. Otherwise tensions in the community would be felt by everyone, just as in families.

One cloudy morning, shortly before Thanksgiving vacation in 1982, just as morning meeting was about to end, Maureen, a staff member, called for a community meeting. She asked that everyone remain because she had a concern that she felt needed to be addressed in a community meeting. The meeting didn't give teachers much time to change their plans for classes, but sensing the concern in Maureen's voice, everyone agreed to postpone classes. We took a fifteen minute break, so people could get a cup of tea or go to the bathroom. Then the 23 students and 10 staff members returned to the circle.

All of our meetings were held in the common room in the Yellow House. The room was 20'x30', with a fireplace and wood stove on one side, and a large picture window, which faced out to the front of the house, on the other. Looking southeast out this window one had a framed view of Mt. Carr.   On the northeast end were two more windows and a door leading out to a side porch which wrapped around to the front of the house. The only piece of furniture in the room was the old but playable upright piano which we had bought early on for about $25. The rest of the room was covered with colorful pillows of all sizes and shapes resting on top of a thick plush chocolate brown carpet. This was our main meeting room for all school events from music and skit night to morning meetings to the meeting that was now about to happen.

Some people rested against the pillows, some leaned against each other, and some sat cross-legged on pillows. I could feel the tension in the room. Community meetings usually were about serious stuff – big issues. A chipped coffee cup rested on the floor in front of Maureen. The cup would serve as our talking cup. At the last minute someone had grabbed the cup from the kitchen which was right off the common room to the rear. The BRS tradition was to "pass the cup" (which in other traditions might be referred to as "passing the talking stick") around the room; whoever held the cup was the one who had the floor. If you had something to say, you had to wait till the cup came to you.

Maureen began the meeting by picking up the cup and speaking firmly. "I've been feeling overwhelmed in the past two weeks. Many of you have not been showing up for cook or work crew or doing your homework. Last night I was on cook crew and two of you never showed up. That rarely happens. So Mary and I scrambled to prepare the meal on time not knowing whether the rest of the crew would show up or not. And then at the last minute as everything was being put out on the serving tables in the dining room, the two other crew members showed up all apologetic. I felt annoyed, so of course I am wondering what is going on. I know in the past whenever drugs are present in this community, we lose our connection and the drugs interfere with our functioning so that is why I'm bringing up the subject now. It's just a hunch. Whether the culprit is drugs or not, whatever is going on, we need to talk about it."

She looked around at the group. Her voice softened as she said, "I love you all so much and it hurts me when I can't trust you. I imagine you might feel the same when you feel you can't trust me or other staff members. Trust is so important in this community."

Unhesitant, she passed the cup on to the person next to her. I could feel my heart beat increase. I took a long slow breath, and told myself to relax. I could hear the voice within me saying "Here we go, another long one", but I also felt confident that as with all of our past community meetings, by just giving people a safe structure in which to talk and feel, we would come out stronger and closer. This was not about confessions and punishments. This was about a community talking to each other from an honest place and if the subject turned out to be drugs, then drugs were to be our teacher.

The cup passed silently around the circle, each member choosing not to respond to Maureen's challenge right away. With no one speaking to the problem the tension in the room mounted. I could feel my own muscles tighten, especially in my legs. They always start to quiver when I get scared. I had to keep taking long breaths to relax them. I'm not a great fan of conflict and although I knew that in the past our group process had strengthened our bond as a community the fear of not knowing what would unfold in this meeting was there.

I was reminded that in my family growing up we had, of course, never dealt with conflict. In fact, I thought back then that there wasn't any conflict. I never realized all the turmoil I was experiencing as a child and never talked about was actually conflict. There was no acknowledged conflict because no one ever talked about my father's drinking, or my father's affair or anything. (A friend of my mother's had told me a few years after my mother died that when my mother found out about my father's affair, she never confronted him in person. She wrote him letters even though they lived in the same house).

Silently the cup continued to move around the circle from person to person with no mention of drugs. I continued to listen with curiosity and apprehension as each member of the community very gingerly and cautiously accepted the cup as it was handed to them knowing that they had the choice to either pass it on to the next person or share what they knew or felt about the issue at hand. When the cup came to me, I also chose to pass it without saying anything. I wanted to give students an opportunity to speak and be heard before I did.

Finally, Sandra broke the silence. With her knees drawn to her chin and her hands clutching her legs, she let go of her legs and with one hand awkwardly accepted the cup. She looked down at the floor and said in a shaky voice, "I hate it when I see my friends breaking rules because I know that no matter what I say it doesn't matter." She lifted her teary eyes looking out the window at the end of the room toward fields and ever-present Mt. Carr. Still not making eye contact with anyone and continuing to look out the window, she said, "I really care about everyone here and I'm afraid of losing you. I don't know what to do so I don't do anything. And it's scary to even share this with you."

She quickly passed the cup to Janet without looking at anyone. As Sandra settled back into a more relaxed position on her cushions, Louise, who had chosen not to talk, sitting on the other side of her, reached out and put her arm around her shoulders, giving her a quick squeeze indicating that she understood her and perhaps felt the same way. I was thinking how gutsy that had been of Sandra to share that.

Janet, relaxed, and comfortable, sitting on top of some soft yellow pillows leaning against the pale yellow wall of the common room in one quick smooth movement, took the cup from Sandra, sat straight up and tossed her head back. It seemed clear that she had connected with Sandra's feelings. She sat there quietly for a few moments, and then deliberately turned her gaze toward each of us. Her mouth and brow tightened. She looked annoyed. "The only people who have any power to do anything here are the staff. That makes me angry. I feel powerless and scared like Sandra to say anything to anybody because if I do, I'm afraid I will be not only misunderstood but not accepted by my friends. I know how Sandra feels. That makes me not want to say anything either."

As the angry tears came she passed the cup along to the next person.

She's right on, I thought to myself. How scary to even think of losing your friends by telling on them. And to wonder what is tattle tailing and what is sharing information. After all, what could be more important than your friendships?

The cup kept moving around but with not too much response. Then Jennifer spoke up, her voice sounding impatient and frustrated. She said "I have to admit that it bugs me that so many of you are passing the cup without talking. Like always, the same people are doing the talking and I'm usually one of them. But today, I want to hear what everyone is thinking". Yay, Jennifer, I thought to myself.

I also was usually one of those people who spoke up a lot in this community and often felt annoyed at those who did not speak up, including Bruce, when I knew he had to have a lot of thoughts and feelings but wasn't speaking up. That would trigger me maybe because I never dared to speak up in my family. Now I just went along with the silence.

Jennifer happened to be sitting next to Karen, who was one of those silent ones. As Karen rather timidly received the cup from Jennifer, she said,"I feel frustrated also but with myself because I don't say anything. I'm really afraid that what I say in this group isn't important or doesn't matter anyway. I hate that about myself but that has been my experience since I can remember at home and at my old school. Don't get involved was the message. Best to keep your feelings and thoughts to yourself and not talk so I don't."

Making eye contact with only the floor, she slowly slid the cup across the floor where it rested in front of Sonia, one of our seasoned staff members. I thought to myself again: "That too was gutsy. You, Karen, are being so courageous right now and I totally understand what you are saying from the perspective of when I was your age." I never said anything in school for fear someone would be judging what I was saying as unimportant or of no value. I knew in my family not to speak up because someone was certainly going to disagree or tell me my point of view was the wrong one. I basically shared nothing and eventually I believed I had nothing worth saying.

Sonia picked up the cup, and for a few moments, she said nothing. There was silence in the room. Her eyes focused on the cup. Tenderly she moved her finger around the ridge of the cup stopping for a moment to notice the chipped area and then moving her finger around again. Eventually she broke the silence, moved her focus from the cup to Karen and in a soft and tender voice said, "Thank you for taking the risk to share that piece of you, Karen. I want you to know how much I love you and I really want to know what you feel and think. That is very important to me, and I hope you will share more." Hearing that, Karen began to cry responding with,

"Thank you. That really means a lot." I could always count on our staff to validate and appreciate the students and I felt very proud of Sonia's comments towards Karen.

Then Jen spoke up. She said. "I confess that I have been smoking cigarettes, but I didn't know anyone cared that much. I have so many good friends here but I don't think I can give up smoking. I try to smoke away from people. I'm really addicted to smoking and I don't know if I can stop." Hesitantly, she passed the cup on.

After a few more passes of the cup, people began to open up more. Perhaps some like Kevin and Pete felt inspired or moved by what others had said before them and now felt safer and less apprehensive to speak.

Then Kevin shared. "I feel very nervous talking about drugs because my brother's best friend overdosed and died and nobody ever talked about it. This is the first time I've ever said anything about it and I don't feel comfortable doing this. I realize I have a lot of feelings." His voice began to choke up but he quickly got a hold of himself and passed the cup on to Pete.

Pete spoke up in a matter of fact tone saying, "My father is an alcoholic, and we don't talk about it, either. In fact I feel embarrassed telling you. My parents would kill me if they knew I was telling you this. We don't talk about my father's drinking or anything that really matters."

When the cup was handed to his roommate John, who up to this point had been in a somewhat carefree repose on the floor, perhaps wondering if taking a little snooze would go unnoticed, abruptly sat up to face Pete. With surprise in his tone of voice he faced Pete and recounted his own story.

"My dad is also an alcoholic but I never wanted anyone to know that because I feel so ashamed." Much to his apparent surprise, his eyes began to tear up. Pete, still triggered and somewhat shocked at telling his story and trying to hold back his tears moved closer to John. He put his arms rather awkwardly around John's shoulders and in a low but audible voice said "I didn't know we had this is common. Maybe we can share some more."

Then Jason, another staff member, shared that his father was also an alcoholic and how his drinking had had such an impact on him when he was little and still did especially when he heard other people's stories about alcohol or drug related incidents. He said that because he could never count on his father being there for him and how the family tiptoed around him, Jason never knew when he would come home drunk and start yelling. He lived in constant anticipation. He said, "I really understand how you, Pete and John must feel."

I could feel the whole group opening up now as James shared the story of his friend being killed in a drug related car accident. He recalled, "I was devastated, but I didn't know how or who to talk to. If people asked me how I was doing I always said 'fine.' I never believed they really wanted to know how I was feeling and to be honest with you, I wasn't sure I knew either. Isn't the manly thing to do is to say "fine? That's what I learned growing up." Now he began to cry at the pain of remembering his friend.

There was an outpouring of empathy in the room. Many people were crying and words of understanding prevailed. Everyone moved closer to one another. Having been a part of the Re-evaluation Counseling community for nearly ten years now, I felt comfortable and encouraged by the outpouring of empathy and caring as did the students and staff.

As I listened to the stories unfold I felt my face begin to blush and my heart open up. I wanted to reach out to everyone. I couldn't help but be reminded of my family and my dad who loved to party and on Saturday night would get drunk and sometimes pass out. And we never talked about it. The same scenario played out at every dinner party, cocktail party, celebration my parents went to, including important events in my life such as holidays, and even my wedding.

I don't know how many times I had sat in my parents' bedroom watching them get dressed for a party, joking with each other and with me, my father clowning around by putting a shirt on backwards or tying his tie some crazy way. I felt so safe watching them playfully tease me and each other but then only to see the same behavior as well as the same results; he got drunk, my mother got mad.

He had a few very good social friends, consisting mainly of six couples. His relationship with them was mostly Saturday night parties along with the wives, lots of alcohol, laughing. The get-togethers had started out with playing bridge every other Saturday night but eventually the bridge ended and the partying took over. These six couples had a wonderful time together. They went on outings, organized skit nights and in general were loyal to each other right up till the time they died. Their lives were strictly social, maybe an occasional golf game but mostly the parties. I loved all the couples and referred to each of them as aunt and uncle. If my parents left any legacy, it was they knew how to have a party and have fun, albeit alcohol dependent. Drinking and smoking and driving a car were benchmarks of adulthood.

Sunday morning was cloaked in silence after a Saturday night party. I usually tried to fix things for my mom because ironically I didn't want her to be mad at him. I couldn't tolerate the conflict between them. So on many occasions I would go into their bedroom, make the beds and straighten things up. Later on in my life, I felt very angry at my father and whenever he had that certain look on his face after a few drinks, I would distance myself from him emotionally, physically, mentally, the same way my mother did. I never had a conversation with him about how I was feeling or how his drinking impacted me.

In fact, no one ever addressed how my father's drinking affected the dynamics in our family. My mother ignored the subject, perhaps secretly hoping before each party that this time the outcome would be different. And maybe I was secretly hoping for the same outcome as I sat on my mom's bed listening to them get ready to go out. Maybe tonight would be different.

But no words were ever spoken.

At age sixteen, I had my first "legal" drink meaning I could drink with my family. I also could "legally" smoke in the family. My mom and dad smoked Phillip Morris cigarettes and on different tables throughout the house were glass cigarette holders filled with cigarettes alongside a silver cigarette lighter, the kind Bruce and I received for wedding presents. Drinking and smoking cigarettes were common practices in my family and in the families of ninety percent of my friends. I had a few friends who didn't smoke or drink but I couldn't understand why they didn't. Was there something wrong with them? Smoking and drinking determined our passage from adolescence to adulthood. It defined our maturity. Cocktail parties were for adults. Marlboros, gin and tonics, bourbon mists permeated my life for twenty years.

Now as I listened here to all these young people talk about their situations with friends and family, I realized that not much had changed.

After several short breaks in the morning and then an hour or so break for lunch, we continued into the afternoon. It was then that Joe acknowledged with great remorse that he had brought some pot back after a weekend at home. He had no idea that doing so would have such an effect on the community and he regretted doing so.

I felt sad as I looked at Joe. When the cup came to me I said, "I am sorry that you didn't understand how important you are and how loved and respected you are in the community and how much we need your leadership?" I listed his strengths and all the contributions he had brought to the community. I could feel my tears rising. I said I was sorry not to have told him before. He started to cry saying he didn't feel important and didn't know he made a difference to any adults. He started sharing times in his life when he felt deceived by broken promises, a time when he was nine or ten and his father had promised to take him to the traveling circus that was coming through town, but on the day he was to take him, a business crisis came up and he couldn't go. When Joe had started to cry, he had been chastised for not being understanding and more cooperative. Situations like this with his dad had accumulated. I felt sad and angry about what had happened to Joe.

In that moment I felt such love and appreciation for these young people. And so I told them that their honesty and openness made us feel so much closer to them. We wanted them to know that their actions did indeed affect everyone the same way our actions or inactions affected them. Having shared my thoughts and feelings and having seen the students' expressions of love and appreciation, I suddenly felt more connected and relaxed, and passed the cup.

I knew my message of love for them had been communicated and received. Every staff member at that meeting, through their openness to show students their pain and feelings, also showed them how much they cared about each one of them.

And so, even though nothing specific had yet been decided, the simple sharing by all had multiplied feelings of relaxation and safety, and clarity and space was opening up for what needed to happen. When we took a longer break again in mid-afternoon, the day had become appropriately clear and sunny. I decided to hike the hill to stretch my legs and get some fresh air before we reconvened. Others joined in.

As we walked I thought: regardless of what action we take here, we might not be able to get rid of drugs for good, but at least we can create a community whose members can talk to each other and share their thoughts and feelings embedded in stories that had never been processed.

When we returned, a motion was made by Bruce during the afternoon that took many by surprise. The school was scheduled to close for Thanksgiving break in three days. He proposed that we close the school the following day, with the stipulation that all students go home, that everyone, staff included, think about what an honest trusting community meant to them and how committed they were to each other and to the policies and philosophy of the school. He was, in effect, saying that everyone in the community needed to share responsibility for the several school policy violations that had emerged from the meeting, not just those who had come forward, and that everyone also needed to take responsibility for the future of the school if it was to continue. He was proposing to lay the school on the line for everyone.

Everyone reacted. Many fears were expressed; fears of the school closing permanently; fears of returning to old schools; fears of losing friends and what it would mean to give up BRS. The cup went around the room quite a few times more. But, in the end, everyone agreed to an early Thanksgiving closing of BRS the next day.

Out of the meeting it was clear that commitment and trust had emerged as the major issue and many were facing it head on for the first time, realizing their individual responsibility for keeping the community strong and viable.

Immediately after the meeting, which actually took us into the evening hours, students called their parents and made arrangements for leaving. The following day, as agreed upon, everyone, including the staff, was assigned the task of writing a letter during the time away, to arrive by the day after Thanksgiving, confirming their intention to make a recommitment to the policies and to the community. If a student chose not to write a letter, then she or he was choosing not to return to school.

My immediate task after the closing of the meeting was to write to parents. Part of that letter included the following thoughts:

A new form of support and care and power seem to be happening for all of us here. Although it will take time for trust to develop again when we return, there is a feeling of love and strength that existed here today that I have never experienced before. I wish all of you could have been here with us. Our 'system' does so little to help young people connect with their power and authenticity that it is little wonder we only see potential in young people. Drug use is a symptom of this powerlessness, lack of self worth, and helplessness, that so many feel. We have only to look back on our own experience as young people to know that those feelings are not new to our children or to look at the abuse of drugs in our own families and all around us to know that feelings and addictions also pass down from generation to generation.

The staff feels very proud of what has happened in the last few days and feels a strong commitment to your child. The same commitment must come from the students. Our jobs are not separate from our lives. We love one another very deeply and the meeting provided us with the space to express that love. We are all feeling more powerful.

The staff remained at school to answer questions parents had concerning this series of events and to lend support to each other. We were grateful that the parents were as usual very supportive and their trust reassured us.

As the letters arrived during the next few days, we posted them on the board. Here are a couple of samples.

One first-year senior wrote:

Now I know why I chose BRS for my senior year. The reason is because a safety exists for me there that has never existed here at "home". At BRS I am part of a community, not just one of the kids. I can speak my mind without fear of being yelled at or punished. I want that kind of safety for every person there and realize now after ten or so hours of meeting how much my actions affect others. I'm trying to deal with some strong guilt feelings that say it will be hard to go back. People won't like you. You don't deserve to be there. But part of me reminds me of all the good and growth that's come out of my three or so months at BRS and I realize I'll just have to deal with the guilt and so what is best for me which is to return. I told myself that if I break a policy upon my return or fail to bring up any knowledge I may have of broken commitments then my commitment to the community is not strong enough to warrant being there. I know I'll need support and also NO TEMPTATIONS. If I confess for you realize it is because I care and because I'm afraid of what I may do before I even think about it. I love you all. See you in a week.

A second year staff member wrote:

Dear friends, when I first learned about BRS. I couldn't believe it really existed. It was the kind of place I had fantasized about working in, but I had always thought I would have to settle for something less. Here was a school that embodied values that are important to me, a community and an environment that spoke to me of a healthy and sane approach to the world.

In all of my thinking in the past about what I wanted to do with life was the knowledge that I wanted to be involved in social change. I decided that as an educator I could combine a lot of my interests and goals. I sought training in order to be as effective in my role as possible. And here I found a school that was bringing about the changes that were important to me: changes in the way we communicate with each other, changes in the way men and women relate, in the way adults and young people relate, in the way we relate to society as powerful human beings and in the way we relate to the natural world. I know that this school was where I could find my niche.

If we want to change the world, we've got to begin with ourselves. This is a place where people can have the love and support not to hurt them. This is a place where we can trust each other enough to give that support and to ask for it when we need it. That trust is so unique and so valuable. I want to trust that people will do what's right for themselves, that they won't hurt themselves or others.

Drugs really aren't the main issue here, they are merely a symptom. But they are something I wanted to speak to, in order to illustrate what it means to make a commitment. That is the issue, trust and commitment. Those two go hand in hand. The bottom line is that you can't fully commit yourself to something unless you believe in it.

I am deeply committed to this community, this school and the ideals it is built upon. We can change the world and we are doing it by learning to love one another and learning to love ourselves.

One staff member's retreat

Chapter Nine

COMMUNITY JOURNAL

A community journal was kept on a shelf alongside our only telephone. When someone walked into the Yellow House from the glassed-in porch (the "mud room"), the telephone and the journal were the first items they would see. Anyone could write in the journal at any time and write whatever was on their mind. If you wanted to know what a teenager thought from day to day, the journal said it all. What was important to me was that they risked sharing their feelings and thoughts with the whole community. These were not just excerpts from private journals, but self-revelations for all to read. Some were signed and others not. Here are some sample entries exactly how they appeared in the journal but without names attached.

> I spend lots of time in my room reading. I'm not sure some people really want to be with me. I get really afraid when I like someone a lot that I'll do something weird or stupid or something like that. Like part of growing older is that you learn not to trust that people care about you. So when I trust people before I know them really well, let my guard down that I'm being really naïve because of course they are going to hurt me – almost like a formula. Trust=naïve which leads to hurt. Bummer, huh? Like

people are just humoring me by being with me. It feels weird because the desire to trust and care and love and let people inside comes naturally but I suppress it so I won't get hurt. Am I repeating myself? Am I repeating myself ha ha ha. That's all. It's not but that's all for here. I want to write to each person a note but I don't. I do but I won't.

Articulation is really weird. Why do some people feel like they can't ever express their feelings well enough? It sure isn't because they aren't able to. People know what I mean.

Hi, I feel like YELLING laughing ... Crying screaming I'm full of it.

Snow and rain force me to cuddle, huddle near the warmth of a burning fire. Confused, anxious, I cower behind the protection of the TIMES hoping that somehow I will be able to cry

If you need help come to me. I'm here. I want to help.

I'm telling you jealousy is the worst thing alive on this earth. It hurts and I want to just love people and not have to sit burning up inside. It SUCKS I realize how long it's has been since I've really loved people – well it's not that way at all I just plain and simply hate the feeling called JEALOUSY. Well, I must admit, I've come along way.

————- What happened? You are not the same. Is it something I did? I want to talk to you.

Why is it so hard? And why am I sad? And why do I cry alone in a small room with my face in a pillow to choke the scream which wells up from inside, gushing into the darkness. So alone....It would be so much easier to give in, to give up, Right now I can't recall why I continue to struggle.

I went ice skating today. It was such fun. To skate and open my arms like I'm flying. I love to glide. Zoom like a zoomer. I would love to wear a big cape and skate and let it flap behind me. I really would love to skate with everyone but there are not enough skates. The snow is incredibly bright. I can't wait to ski. I love everyone....

We share in our fears of being caged. We share in knowing we are free. I can feel your struggle in trying to make your words just right in your writing in the other journal. It was wonderful. Our words are wonderful. Everything about us is wonderful. We are so scared of being imperfect and in our fight to be perfect we don't ever see what we have become.

You've been on my mind quite often lately. I've found out some s—- that didn't settle too easy inside. I've been seeing your anger a real lot lately and I feel sure it is towards me. I was thinking we should get together with a third party this week and have a gab, release of anger etc. session. It would do us both good I feel. I have a feeling I could get you angry enough to get it out. I remember you said you were having a hard time. Don't take this sarcastically. Know I'm thinking about you. I do care.

Ya_____let's do it up. I don't feel mad, just kind of hurting inside. Thanks.

It was wonderful walking out onto the salt marsh yesterday. Everyone was so excited. It's so neat to teach people who are so excited. Hermit crabs. A dead skate. Crabs. Shells. Sun. Reflections. Rainbow cloud. I feel very good about my teaching too. I'm getting a lot closer to people and it feels good. Boy, I wish my teachers in high school had been able to hug me the way I love to hug these students.

Chapter Ten

THE KITCHEN AS THE CENTER OF THE COMMUNITY

"Only in a prosperous society could we ever forget that food is one of life's primary blessings." - John Robbins, *Diet for a New World*

Every aspect of the kitchen and our relationship to food was central to our philosophy: knowing the food and its sources; knowing how to prepare it and how critical our eating patterns were to our survival and well being; in short, everything I never learned growing up. The BRS kitchen came to serve as a place to understand the connection between feelings and food, namely the understanding that food was also a drug: and how its quality and content had profound effects on our mental and physical health and our ability to concentrate, focus, feel sharper and experience our aliveness

As a community we were all, staff and students, responsible for the preparation, cooking and serving of three meals a day plus cleaning the kitchen after meals, the daily baking of bread plus two early morning trips a week to the bottom of the hill to pick up our weekly dairy supplies which were delivered there.

I found those cold dreary winter mornings when I had to get up early to go over to the Yellow House for breakfast duty very challenging. It was still dark outside and the wood stove located in the basement of the Greenhouse had not yet been fed its morning supply of wood to heat up the house. On other mornings, I could turn on the space heater, jump back into bed and in no time feel a warm room. Getting out of bed was not a problem.

Incidentally, my possession of a space heater was sometimes a bone of contention with students. How come I had special privileges they didn't have, like having a space heater? I responded by blaming it on menopause and the fact that I got colder more easily than they did. After all, there had to be some privileges that came with menopause.

I remember one typical cold wintry morning, climbing out of my warm cozy comfortable bed, imagining how it must be for a caterpillar to leave the safety and warmth of its cocoon. But very reluctantly I managed to drag myself out from underneath my warm quilt and one by one placed my feet on the cold floor. My eyelids struggled to stay open as I fought that strong part of me that wanted to jump back into bed. The room temperature was probably about 45 degrees. I moved quickly, flung off my long flannel night shirt, and with a shiver slipped into my cold jeans, turtle neck and heavy sweater.

(We all dressed for warmth and comfort, not in the latest fashions. I bought most of my clothes at a thrift store in Plymouth and I loved dressing comfortably and informally).

I began to warm up as one by one I slipped my arms into my most recently acquired thrift store purchases: my down jacket, which on cold mornings felt more like a life jacket. I moved down the squeaky wood stairs to the first floor as quietly as possible so as not to wake up others, grabbed my scarf from my cubby next to the front door, and tossed it around my neck and slowly made my way out the door into the cold morning air. There was enough light from the early dawn for me to find my way past the dumpster and the barn across the road to the Yellow House to meet the rest of the kitchen crew.

By the time I reached the kitchen I was fully awake. Two of the other cook crew members were already there. I noticed Josh was in the common room right off the kitchen putting more logs in the wood stove. The job of morning kitchen crew was also to stoke the two wood stoves, one in the common room and the other in the dining room/ library area. "What's for breakfast?" I yelled out to him. "Look at the menu board", he yelled back. The menu board hung on the wall just as you came into the kitchen. Meals were posted there for the week so anyone could decide whether they wanted to come to breakfast or not. As Josh was stoking the fire, the dairy crew was just returning from their twice-weekly early morning hike down the hill to meet the dairy truck. They were laughing and joking around, obviously wide awake from the brisk air and the invigorating walk up and down the hill. They proceeded to unload their backpacks filled with the milk, yogurt, cheese, butter, eggs, and other supplies for the next few days. Unlike the rest of our food orders from other sources, which were picked up in town by our truck on a weekly basis, this order required prompt pickup.

The menu this morning was homemade muffins and granola, fruit salad, and yogurt. Sometimes we made our yogurt but mostly yogurt was store bought. My job this morning was the salad: cut up oranges, apples, mixed with grapes, and bananas. It was the oranges that took the time.

All meals were served buffet style in the dining room, so when people were hungry, getting to the head of the line could be an issue for some, depending on the menu, of course. Breakfast, though, was not so crazy. Unlike lunch and dinner typically filled with noisy clatter, here students quietly shuffled into the dining room, not yet awake enough to get feet completely off the ground. With half a smile and a barely audible "hello", students loaded their plates from the assortment of breakfast goodies.

Thus do I remember the kitchen at breakfast.

From my records and journals, I recently found this typical weekly breakfast menu:

Monday: Scrambled eggs. Toast, homemade granola and yogurt
Tuesday: Oatmeal, toast, granola, yogurt
Wednesday: Fresh baked muffins, fruit salad, granola, yogurt
Thursday: French toast, granola, yogurt
Friday: Oatmeal, muffins, granola, yogurt
Saturday: fried eggs, coffee cake (homemade) granola, and yogurt
Sunday: blueberry pancakes (our own berries), maple syrup (also our own) granola, yogurt

For lunch there was usually homemade soup, such as vegetable, tomato, squash, or onion. The weekly lunch menu I found from the same records included: make-your-own sandwiches (egg salad, cheese or tuna), homemade bread fresh from the oven, leftovers from the previous night's dinner, fruit salad, fruit, cut up carrots, celery sticks, coleslaw, and, as always, a huge salad.

The dinner menu for the same week included tofu casseroles, vegetarian chili, lasagna, and stir fry veggies with tofu. And yes, a large salad.

We ate lots of pasta and beans. Occasionally we served chicken. Our milk, as noted, came from a local dairy. Many of our other bulk products and much fresh produce came from a recently organized community food co-op in a nearby town. For sweetener, we replaced sugar with honey from a local beekeeper and maple syrup from our own sugaring operation. Although we acted as models for healthy eating (as we understood the word "healthy" back then) it didn't mean that on town trips, students couldn't eat what they wanted. As a school, though, we wanted to be the model.

One of the first things a visitor might see when entering the BRS kitchen when it was not being used would be its bright blue walls, its red and white checkered curtains, and next to the sinks several drying racks holding large quantities of yellow plates, bowls, silverware, small and large cutting boards, pans, buried under another layer of bread pans, cooking pots, strainers, pitchers, flat pans, large and small baking dishes. These racks covered about four feet of counter space and rising vertically blocked out half the light from the window next to the sink.

This cleanup scene that generated this picture repeated itself three times a day. Everything was washed by hand and rinsed twice before set out to dry. This was because the New Hampshire Department of Health required that every dish and every utensil air dry. It was against health regulations to towel dry. So that's how we did it: one washer and one rinser for every meal. Cleaning up after every meal was quite a project but everyone in the community took on this job at least two or three times a week, and it was "mission accomplished" after every meal (unless someone occasionally forgot, which definitely created a problem).

If a guest were to visit the kitchen on a Wednesday afternoon, which was work crew afternoon, he or she would see every inch of counter space taken up with all the contents from the two refrigerators and from the large open shelves located on both sides of the large two-oven Magic Chef commercial stove. The shelves were lined with large two-gallon jars obtained from the local food co-op. Each jar contained bulk food such as rice, lentils, beans, dried peas, spices, noodles, and dried fruit.

As I looked up at these jars on any given day when I was in the kitchen, I was struck by how beautiful food is in its natural state, and how each of these foods has its own shape and color. One of our staff, Margie, was a skilled calligrapher, and her carefully scribed labels on each container added to the overall beauty and elegance of the picture. In most kitchens food is tucked away under counters behind doors and never to be seen until it appears on the plate, but in our kitchen, the food was on exhibit.

The Wednesday afternoon kitchen cleaning also involved replenishing containers as needed from supplies in our adjacent storeroom. Also, the refrigerators and the shelves were scrubbed, scoured, and wiped clean. The crew did whatever it took to get the job done, always with music from a portable tape player. What kind of music depended on who was on kitchen crew on that day. It could be anything from blues to folk to country to rock n' roll, and even classical (rarely).

Two hours later, the kitchen would be back in perfect order, every shelf immaculate, every inch of the stove top and ovens spotless, the refrigerators freed of any lingering inedible. And although the floor was mopped as part of every evening cleanup, on Wednesday it got special treatment beyond the mopping. Maybe some wax. Many a time I was down on my hands and knees waxing the floor, usually a task I took on during holiday vacations.

Actually, this was one of the work crew tasks I rarely signed up for. I had had enough kitchen duty in my own home over the years, so that I had a tendency to avoid it and the kitchen in general, other than for my scheduled cooking assignments.

I did like organizing in other areas of the school and I was good at it. Growing up, I had often complained to myself about my mother and how organized she was. Things got picked up and put away even before I finished using them. If I poured myself a cup of tea and then went to the bathroom, I would for sure take the tea with me because if I didn't, it might be gone by the time I returned. But her sense of organization and management did serve me and the BRS community well.

It showed up in my self-designated task in the first year to create enough space in the common room to comfortably seat 30 or more people. Since the furniture that was left in the common room by the previous tenants was less than desirable, I had no problem moving all the pieces into the barn. Having emptied out the room of all furniture except the piano tucked into one corner, I decided to furnish the common room with pillows - at least 50 of them – to rest on top of a very comfortable, thick chocolate brown colored wall-to-wall carpet. I had gone on a campaign to find pillows whether they were at yard sales or the second hand thrift store 50 cent special. I found them wherever I could and then I went looking for material and one by one eventually covered every pillow. The walls in the common room were lined with pillows of all shapes, sizes and colors Each summer, I dismantled all the covers, washed them and sewed them back on again - nothing fancy, no zippers or anything like that. I cut up old clothes, slipcovers, and end pieces from the fabric stores. One summer, I painted the common room walls yellow and made simple curtains for the two windows on the northeast side of the room. So the room felt very open and looked very bright and cheerful.

In addition to the piano in the common room, there was actually one table next to the entry. If I hadn't kept a close eye on it, it would easily have become the junk table. It was amazing how, as the only empty surface available, it drew all sorts of things to it. My solution was to put anything I found that didn't belong there into a lovely antique "junk" box right next to it. In that box you could find any-thing from text books, socks, knitting needles, note pads, sweaters to hair brushes, combs, head bands, and hats.

I often wondered what that table would have looked like if I hadn't cleared it off every day. So if anyone asked "Do you know where my _____is?" I just pointed to the box.   But I liked jobs like this: organizing, dusting, vacuuming, and sweeping.

I also liked to stack wood. There was always a need for someone to do that since we harvested and worked up 20 cords of wood every year, wood that needed to be stacked in different locations convenient to each building. Every fall the whole community was involved in the many chores of getting ready for winter.

But to return to the kitchen: If a guest visited there right after morning meeting, he or she would be greeted by the bread makers for the day. This was also an assigned duty. And since fresh bread would be needed for lunch, the bakers needed to begin the dough as early as possible. Although some students or staff knew the recipe by heart, others like me would probably have page 32 of *The Vegetarian Epicure* opened to directions for whole wheat bread. This page was easy to find, marked and dirty as it was from many wet doughy hands of bread bakers and from penciled instructions in the margins for how to quadruple the recipe. It was basically a simple recipe using milk, butter, salt, honey, yeast, wheat germ, wheat flour, and of course copious amounts of whole wheat flour. The bread bakers would chat away as they kneaded, punched, pulled and squeezed the wet sticky dough through their hands until it was manageable enough to move into a large buttered bowl covered with a damp towel and left ready to rise.

Since the bread was necessary for lunch, the bakers would need to return at some later time in the morning between classes, to knead it again, form it into loaves, put the loaves into bread pans, and put into the ovens in time to be ready for lunch. Every student and staff learned how to bake bread.

On one occasion during the sexuality unit of the Health and Well-Being module, when we had a visitor at one of our lunches, I noticed something strange about the loaves being served. They looked different, not the usual shape of the bread. I didn't think much about their shape at first. It was one of those partially unconscious moments when I noticed something was different but didn't give too much attention to it. Then, suddenly I realized that the bread bakers that morning had shaped each loaf into the form of a penis. I don't think our guest noticed. I wasn't sure about his sense of humor, but I was chuckling inside.

Our main bible for recipes at BRS was *Diet for a Small Planet*, by Frances Moore Lappe, published in 1971. This book was more than a cookbook, and represented some of newest thinking about food at the time. This book was a textbook in many ways, proposing that protein from plants is just as valuable as protein that comes from meat. Lappe wrote:

This book is about protein, how we as a nation are caught in a pattern that squanders it, and how we can choose the opposite; namely, a way of eating that makes the most of the earth's capacity to supply this vital nutrient.

Actually this book was also important to us from a practical stand point because we couldn't afford meat. We needed to find alternatives, and one of the people living in the Yellow House the year before the opening of the school had discovered this book. Enter tofu into our lives. What a shock! I mean, what is a meal without meat? When my kids had asked me what was for dinner, my answer was basically either "pork chops", "meat loaf", or "chicken". Every main meal had been defined by the meat. Now, we would be saying "tofu!"

At first we did everything to disguise it, this gelatin-like white mass of tasteless squirmy nothing. We mashed it; we mixed it with veggies; we cut it up in small bite like pieces and marinated it in sauces, and then stir fried it.

In sum, learning about food and how to cook became an integral part of living in our BRS community. The kitchen was the busiest, most used, most important and, along with the common room, most central space in the whole house. Eating was a time of celebration of coming together as a community to have fun, share, talk with your friends, and make plans for the rest of the day and to appreciate the cooks and the food. This is the way I thought it should be. Food brought the community together closely three times a day for everyone to connect safely and enjoyably with each other.

This was a radical departure from everything I had learned, assumed, and experienced both growing up in my family and also as a housewife and mother. I carried from growing up the belief that food was about taste. It was about soothing myself when I didn't feel good or filling up when I felt hungry. I learned nothing about its value as a source of essential nutrients and vitamins, where it came from, or how to prepare it. Thus, the message was that nutrition was a topic that had no value and was not important for me to learn about.

How to cook and prepare food had no value either, nor by extension did the person who did the cooking have much value. Cooking and eating were obvious necessities of life but in my family the preparation was hired out to someone outside the family, a maid. This was symbolic of wealth and success.

And as a housewife, I had accepted that the kitchen was a woman's place and that the job of women was to manage the kitchen as well as change the diapers and raise the children. Ever since I had been a little girl playing with my dolls and doll houses, I had looked forward to being that housewife and mother. Even though my mother lacked cooking skill or imagination and could delegate it to Ada, I had seen my mother's role as the one responsible for the kitchen, and that fulfilling this responsibility represented the fulfillment of my potential as a woman. I had never imagined that in fulfilling this role, doing what society had designated and defined for me, would slowly over time wear me down.

Also in my early life it was implicit that the kitchen was a place where women had to take charge, because men simply couldn't. Do you remember the story I told earlier about eating on Ada's day off? On that occasion my mother, who usually prepared my father's breakfast and lunch every day, was not at home, so my father was forced to prepare his own lunch. I happened to be walking through the kitchen and found him heating a can of chicken noodle soup by putting the whole unopened can in a pan of boiling water. How sad that in his lifetime, he had never learned even this simplest of procedures! Even now this is sad to me, especially in that he went through his lifetime thinking that it wasn't even important for him to know how to heat up soup, let alone learn anything about the relationship between food and his health.

All this was the legacy that was passed down to me through my family and which I so completely interrupted.

Although we were far from fully enlightened when it came to our knowledge about food, and what I know now, 26 years after the closing of BRS, it was a beginning of a new consciousness for all of us. We had definitely turned the corner on our eating patterns, developing menus with a strong emphasis on vegetables and fruits when available, if also a little too heavy on the carbohydrates and diary. We knew that we couldn't change overnight. Meat just became less and less a part of the school menu with each succeeding year, as new recipes replaced the old, while at the same time making cooking and preparation of food the responsibility and job of everyone in the community, including parents and other visitors.

To recognize and emphasize both the sense of community and the importance of food, we also started every dinner meal with a circle in the common room. Before a moment of silence, holding hands, we would all sing the well-known Shaker song *Simple Gifts*:

'Tis the gift to be simple, 'tis the gift to be free,
'Tis the gift to come down where we ought to be,
And when we find ourselves in the place just right,
It will be in the valley of love and delight.

When true simplicity is gained,
To bow and to bend we will not be ashamed,
To turn, turn will be our delight,
Till by turning, turning we come out right.

Early morning dairy trip

Loading dairy supplies for the uphill trip

Midway up the hill with dairy supplies

Chapter Eleven

THE POND

We lived on 112 acres of woodlands and streams and open fields and in the center of it all lay my beloved pond, a source of entertainment in all seasons and a source of learning for Biology students especially in the spring. I always wanted to live near water; I think Bruce and I were some type of fish in our past lives. We love to swim and just be near water. The water was spring-fed and fairly clear. No matter where you were you could always see to the bottom, which in the middle of the pond was actually only about eight feet deep. The shore line was sandy with only a few small rocks. In the summer we swam laps across the pond.

Our first summer there, we discovered a snapping turtle living under a makeshift dock on the edge of the pond. Peter, one of our staff, donned his diving gear, caught the turtle and removed him to another pond very far away. At least while we were there the turtle never returned. For the next few weeks, I was a little timid about going swimming. I thought, "If there was one, where is the rest of the family?!"

One of my favorite outdoor times at school was when the snow came. On one particular morning soon after Christmas break, the weather prediction was for a foot of snow, perfect for cross country skiing, which we could do right out our front door. At about eleven o'clock in the morning I began to notice the clouds rolling in over Carr Mountain. We watched with anticipation and excitement as gradually some flakes began to fall. Within a short time the flakes began to turn into larger flakes and heavier snow. Within the hour the ground was covered in white and the snow kept on coming. This was the first major snow of the season. Everyone greeted its arrival with cheers and excitement. When there wasn't any snow in the winter we were like a school without a gymnasium, because we counted on the snow for cross country skiing and sliding down the hill on anything that would slide. Students even slid on top of laundry bags filled with a week or two of laundry on the way to Plymouth and the laundromat every Saturday morning.

Fortunately the pond had frozen solid before the snow came so that all that was required for skating was clearing an area big enough for me to skate a patch. As I looked down at the pond from the green house I noticed that the black ice was beginning to disappear under the flakes. There was probably an inch or so of snow. It was time to bundle up and head for the pond with shovel and skates and my little red stool which I sat on to put on my skates. This little stool had been made by Bruce's younger brother Steve in woodworking class over twenty years earlier and had somehow ended up travelling with us ever since the beginning of our relationship. Both Bruce and I loved to be in the quiet of the snowfall and feel each flake landing on our nose or face. Those moments were magical. Although snow was not deep enough to ski as yet, some students had begun waxing their skis in preparation for the first possible ski of the new winter. Excitement was definitely in the air.

As a child, after a night's snowfall, I had always been the first one in the family to don snowsuit and boots and make the first imprint of an angel in the front lawn of our house. The yard front and back would be covered with angels. I would stay outside until my hands and feet froze and forced me to seek shelter inside. But after everything was dried and I was warmed up out I would go again. As I got older I especially liked snow days when school was cancelled. Hearing the news was like a gift from heaven.

But on this day as the snowflakes slowly drifted down from the heavens, all bundled up in my winter garb I skated out on the ice to clear a patch for myself. Pretty soon, I was joined by others. And the best part of the day lay before us. God bless our beloved pond, I thought.

Betsy's beloved pond

Betsy skating

Swimming in the pond

Chapter Twelve

WOMEN'S EXPEDITION TO THE SOUTHWEST

Note: In this chapter, the names of students have been changed.

On this particular morning during the last year of the school, 1982-83, I woke up feeling anxious and excited. It was February 28, the day Nancy, Kathy, Tara, Sue, Saundra and I were to leave cold New Hampshire for the deserts, mountains, and rivers of Arizona and New Mexico. It had been an uneven winter, and where patches of once white, beautiful flakes of snow covered the ground now lay hard and dirty patches of ice on the frozen ground. I was looking forward to warmer weather.

We had been planning this trip for the past two months, buying and packing food, making clothing and supply lists, planning menus, and plotting our itinerary. Besides our individual equipment lists, we needed group items like tents, tarps for cooking under in rainy weather, stoves, and fuel. Because we would be living in the out-of-doors for the next six weeks, careful planning was essential. Except for some fresh produce and an occasional meal out, we would need to take all our food with us.

One of the students had built a platform for the rear of the blue van and installed it where the back seat had been previously. All of the dry food for six weeks was stored in ziplocked bags under that platform. Another student had built a bookcase in the rear of the van for our many books, literature and maps about the southwest, as well as a roof rack to hold our backpacks and other equipment that wouldn't fit inside the van.

Since January, our group had been meeting often for short periods of time, usually before lunch, to talk about the southwest, the environment, and the climate; to study the map; and to plan our itinerary. We had also talked about possible situations that were apt to arise within the group or with the leaders and how we could handle those. We had read that altitude can affect the way one feels and act and maybe we could get a jump start on those possibilities for disagreements or conflicts by talking about them ahead of time. These were good times together and we were getting to know each other.

But there was a lot I didn't share about my anxiety. I had never done anything as intensive as this before. I had climbed Mt Kearsarge in New Hampshire a few times when I was at summer camp. And with the Hobbit, I had climbed Mt. Carrigain. I had usually been the last one to reach the summit.

Also, every fall we had divided the students and staff into small groups of five or six and begun the school year with our version of Outward Bound as orientation. Those were four to five day trips. My first experience backpacking had occurred as recently as the summer before the school officially opened in 1978. I had never before actually carried a pack on my back, or even spent the night out in the wilderness, carrying food, tent, sleeping bags, and other supplies and equipment. There were three of us: staff member Linda Curran, an experienced outdoorsperson, a visiting friend who had some previous experience, and I. We went off into the White Mountains for three days. As my first experience, I had not found it to be easy, but I had felt good about myself when we returned back to school because I had met my goals.

In this group of students, however, I was definitely the most inexperienced hiker. Having just turned 50, I feared that these young women would be a challenge to keep up with (which eventually proved to be right, but that's getting ahead of my story). During the preparation time, my thoughts often turned to telling myself I was crazy to think I could do this.

I was full of questions for myself. Besides the incentive of wanting to leave cold, dreary New Hampshire, why was I doing this? Was I crazy to think I could even co-lead such an expedition? Did I actually think I could hike down to the bottom of the Grand Canyon and then back up; sleep in a tent or the van for the six weeks in possibly poor weather conditions; eat rice, beans, dried peas, dried fruit, powdered milk, granola, lentils, soup mixes, and gorp every day? Did I really believe that I had enough experience and even the energy to do this journey? Did I want this so badly for myself that I couldn't really see what was going on? Was I denying some of my age old comfort patterns for sleeping, eating and staying warm? What was I thinking or what didn't I want to face about myself?

The rest of the group was extremely responsible, full of adventure and excitement and youthful energy way beyond my comprehension. Maybe, I had convinced myself that age and experience made no difference. But I had been feeling very tired lately. Co-directing the school had been a huge challenge and responsibility. I was already beginning to worry about what we would do for next year. When would there be time to market and recruit BRS students and replace those who would be graduating. Since the world doesn't exactly support this kind of education, I was worried about next year.

Yet, I was tired of winter, working, and just life in general right now. I needed a change. Maybe Kathy and Tara and Sue and Saundra were thinking some of the same thoughts but my perspective of them was that they never tired. They could stay up all night and never get tired. The only thing that tired them out was too much homework. Probably my biggest worry about leading this trip was my lack of experience. I was counting on Nancy to lead us. She was the experienced backpacker, our teacher of environmental science and biology, had led trips in the Grand Canyon and other wilderness areas in the southwest many times before.

And what about being away from Bruce? We rarely had time to interact with each other anyway. I always felt like I was looking at him from a distance. He was living in Moose House, which was way too cold for me, and I was living in my own warm, cozy room in the Green House. Except for my once a week trek over to Moose House to snuggle with him in his bed for a night, time together was a rare. His room was freezing and we huddled in our sleeping bags together with the hoods tightly wrapped around our heads. There was even frost on the inside of the window.

Often in the evening as I walked by the barn I would see him working at his makeshift desk in his makeshift office. There was much to keep up with, paying bills and keeping financial records, since he was solely responsible for the financial end of this operation. I'm sure it was a lonely job at times. During the day, he repaired doors, taught his classes, worked assigned kitchen shifts, and met with students. Since there was very little time for our relationship, going on the expedition would not interfere with that. I often thought to myself that I didn't work nearly as hard as he did.

So here we stood in front of our fully packed blue van on this cold afternoon in February, amid the small patches of old and dirty snow left over from earlier storms. The ground was frozen and hard. The air was crisp and the southwest was looking pretty good to me. The weather forecast was 70 degrees and sunny in Arizona.

The packs were all tied down to the rack on the top of the van, the food was safely secured under the platform in the rear of the van, and coolers were also stowed away. The sun was setting behind Carr Mountain as with big grins on all our faces at last we were ready to climb into the van and say good-bye to BRS, Ellsworth

Hill and other students whose expedition groups were also preparing to leave on their journeys.

Nancy climbed in behind the wheel. Basically, the plan was for Nancy and me to drive non-stop in five or six hour shifts. Kathy, Saundra, Sue, Tara climbed in and took their seats. The most popular place in the van was in the rear over the food because there students could lay out their sleeping bags and sleep if they wanted or just stretch out. That was definitely the best place for sleeping. "Good-bye", we all called out to the others gathered on the stone porch in front of the Yellow House, as we all waved madly back and forth and threw kisses to one another. And so off we went, engine sounding good, with lots of good cheer and excitement inside the van, down the hill on our way to the Southwest.

The long drive from New Hampshire to Arizona went relatively easily. There were times of chatter and times of quiet. We took a southern route down to Oklahoma and then west to New Mexico. One night very late, we stopped by a field and everyone laid out their sleeping bags on the ground and slept for an hour or so.

In three days we arrived at the Superstitions Mountains, during a spring when the desert flowers were in full bloom and the saguaro cacti were responding to their recent soaking. We pulled our van into the head of the Peralta Trail late in the afternoon, unloaded our gear from the roof of the van, and headed off for Fremont Saddle, our first campsite. Here we caught a grand view of Weaver's Needle, a massive high column of rock rising from the desert floor that could be seen from thirty miles away. The rock was soon to develop a special meaning for us.

At night after dinner and clean up we created a ritual of checking in with each other. Everyone was expected to keep a journal of the trip and after dinner became a time to share what we had written or just our thoughts and feelings from the day - what was good and what was hard. It helped keep us in closer contact with each other and everyone seems to look forward to this time.

The night before we reached Weaver's Needle, Saundra, who was 16, had shared how she felt herself beginning to shut down and disconnect from the group. She said she needed help from the group but was not sure what kind of help. She held much anger inside about the abuse she experienced from both her dad and stepdad growing up. Now, the shutting down seemed to be the anger resurfacing. Everyone else also shared their thoughts and feelings.

The next day we arrived at the foothills below Weaver's Needle. As we hiked closer and closer to it, the more its shape seemed to tower over us. Saundra took one look up at this massive piece of rock and as if Weaver's Needle had taken on the powerful image of her two dead fathers, began talking to it.

The talking turned into yelling and crying. With our encouragement, the yelling turned into rage. Her voice echoed throughout the valley. She bellowed up at her father that she was furious because he had abandoned her, and that she refused to any longer be his victim. "I am here and I will not live with this anger and fear any longer," she shouted. "My life is beautiful, and I am beautiful", she yelled. After all the raging and our encouragement, the tears began to subside and a big grin slowly emerged. She was back with us as alive and as beautiful as I have ever seen her.

After Saundra, everyone took the opportunity to let go of some part of their past. Weaver's Needle had become a symbol for all of us. As a result of letting go of so much of our negative energy, we each became spontaneously absorbed in the rest of the day's hike in the beauty of the spring desert: a landscape of cactus, mesquite bush and towering saguaro. Again, I was feeling enormous gratitude for all that Re-Evaluation Counseling had taught me about our healing.

That night Saundra shared the following from her journal.

It was a beautiful day of releasing anger. I almost feel strange. It doesn't feel right somehow to be free of the negativity. I let go of a lot today, but I'm not going to let my father rule my life. When I feel angry at people or feel like I hate them I know it's just because I'm not loving myself, that I'm not living the way I want to.

I can't stand to watch the suffering in the world, old people, loneliness, buildings taking up the freedom of animals and plants. People just won't stop with what they have. Their buildings take over the land forcing animals into cages, and people into office buildings.

After she read her journal, I became aware more than ever what this school was all about. Students were learning an emotional language, and expressing all parts of themselves in their writing and in their talking and sharing.

These young BRS women were so wise in so many ways. To this day, when I hear all the negative talk about teenagers, I think of so many of our BRS students, and their counterparts in the world today. They are waiting for a chance such as our students had to be loved and understood so they can love and understand themselves and then spread all that love out into the world. I was so often impressed with our students' insights and how they were learning to understand the connection between self love and their past histories.

I cannot begin to imagine how my life would have been different if I had been surrounded by adults and teachers who truly loved me enough to believe in me and understand how important it was for me to believe in myself and love me. Saundra really understood the connection between her father's abuse of her and her loving herself, and loving others. I felt so proud of her.

Kathy's journal entry that same night described her day this way.

> Saundra resisted at first but with the help of the group she
> let it out. She screamed, ranted, raved into the hills. She
> made herself known, declared herself. She was beautiful,
> more so than I've ever seen anyone. Her insides tumbled
> out, and her voice was clear, loud, good, unyielding, and
> powerful. Saundra took care of Saundra.

These were the words of another wise and insightful student.

Altogether we hiked six days in the Superstitions. Every day
Nancy taught us much about vegetation and desert ecology. One
day we took a solo day which meant taking a whole day off alone,
reflecting, and writing. There were certain guidelines for how far
away from the campsite to go, so that no one wandered off too far.
This was Kathy's writing from her journal, which she shared in our
group after dinner when we reconnected.

> I'm on a ridge overlooking Weaver's Needle. I'm planted
> on a rock. I hiked up from our new camp where we plan
> to stay until Wednesday. It was scary climbing up there.
> As I went higher and higher my fear grew. What am I
> afraid of? Mostly snakes. I always have my eye out for
> one. Respect is good, but paranoia is more like what I felt.
> Being alone is the flip side of the fear. I feel helpless, pow-
> erless, vulnerable, and superstitious. I wonder if the
> snakes are guarding this natural tower of boulders. Is this
> their sacred palace, a watchtower over the valley? My goal
> was to reach the rock formation at the top. I almost made
> it. But as my fear grew, I realized I needed to stop and
> make friends with the land and its inhabitants. So here I
> am. I keep thinking that I should get up and go .partly out
> of fear. I know I'll feel safe down in camp. It might rain.
> I might get hurt or lost. It might get dark. I could feel
> trapped alone. Somehow I don't feel safe alone. Three

years ago I was all poetry, in a wonder world. Now I find myself wanting to describe, to record what I see, as a naturalist, as if I'd better get it all down on paper so I can go home and draw each dimension, every detail. Am I a greater realist? More aware of the downfalls of life? Wiser for my age or more deadened by it? I don't see this land or myself as poetry now. All I see is what my eyes tell me. I don't feel the colors, the shapes or sounds. I appreciate them. I respect them as whole and true. But at this moment, nothing more.

Going down to read now.

God is with me.

Take a deep breath now. It's yours."

I was taken by the honesty and candor of this young woman's words when she shared them. Her writing showed how much she was growing and pushing through her fears that kept her disconnected from the land.

From the Superstitions, we headed north to the Grand Canyon. This was the part of the trip I looked forward to the most and at the same time felt would be the most challenging. Nancy had our route all laid out for us. We would be descending, then hiking in the floor of the canyon for the next eight days, moving in and out of many smaller canyons. We had to plan how much food to take with us for 24 meals. We had to rearrange our packs because we could only bring in what we could carry on our backs. We had two tents, tarps, cook stoves, fuel, and a first aid kit to carry. We each went over the list of what we needed to include in our packs. Then we distributed the equipment among the six of us. It was clear that the essentials here were a far cry from what we were accustomed to, even back at BRS.

After we were all packed and all the essentials on the list accounted for, we parked and locked up the van, and set out on our first day's trek into the floor of the canyon. I realized after three or four hours of hiking that the descent was a long one, and for every mile down, I would eventually have to hike a mile back up. This was definitely not Mt. Kearsarge. I was feeling a bit overwhelmed. I tried not to think about it.

Everyone did very well on the trip down. We stopped occasionally to administer a band-aid to a blister here and there but we all made it to the bottom fairly easily, including myself. We had hiked long enough now to develop a rhythm as a group and to feel comfortable with each other's pace, though I was as usual at the rear of the group and Nancy at the front.

The first night we set up our tents next to the Colorado River. The banks were sandy and felt comforting to my tired feet. The sounds of the river during the night rocked me to sleep. I felt as if I could have stayed here by the river for a long time.

But the next morning we arose early, folded up our tents, gathered all our gear and headed out to explore the canyon for the next eight days. I felt sad leaving this campsite which was in many ways the best one I had ever camped by.

As the days went by I was growing more and more aware of the feeling of separation I felt from the outside world. As I looked up at the walls of the canyon I felt very far away from civilization. Survival took on more meaning. Here we were all forced to be more conscious of the basic needs of life like the weather, our water and food supply, and dry matches. And of course we needed to be more conscious of how we interacted with the soil, as well as the habitats of snakes and scorpions. We also had to consider that we had to carry out all our trash.

I found myself writing in my journal about how life down here in the canyon wilderness made me feel vulnerable and lonely. I also felt scared at times and as I looked up to the top of the canyon, I wondered how I would be able to climb out. I couldn't seem to bypass those feelings although I tried to distract myself by seeking to connect with the desert floor and the cottonwood trees and fauna and the beauty of it all. I was aware that much of my writing was about my fears and the rest of the group was sharing how in awe they were of the beauty and magnificence of this environment. Here's an entry:

> I like getting up early when the sun is still behind the hills that foreshadow our site. The gradual awakening begins with chirps. The repetition of the sound in the wet crisp air is full of mischief and intrigue. The bird never stops to think. Their world just is. They have nothing to be grateful for, nobody to thank. Their environment is natural and they are a natural link in it. They only depend on us to not interfere. But even as we do, our effect hits and destroys the framework. Unless we become a part of its morning melody, we will totally miss the message.

> We left camp today around 9:15 and hiked three hours into Grapevine Canyon. It was a beautiful hike and at places I could see the Colorado River far below. The color of the canyon rock was red and the hills of the canyon were covered with green bushes and purple prickly pear. One student described it as "a deep warm canyon waiting to fold you up in its hills."

In her journal, Nancy described the Grand Canyon this way:

> New England is my home. It holds my roots. But the southwest is where my branches grow, where my spirit soars. It links with the spirit in the land which is unfettered here. It flies with the raven which is my totem. It sings with the coyote, my sister. I am wild here. I am unfettered. It seems a contradiction but with the scarcity of water

comes a freedom. Just as away from our comfortable civilization there is a freedom. I feel freer here with my backpack and hiking boots.

For eight days we hiked in and out of canyons, taking solo days every once in awhile. I felt anxious to climb out. I was beginning to feel more and more trapped down here. The students, however, continued to hike everyday and with enthusiasm. They were really into it and doing very well.

The day before we were scheduled to make the climb out, we noticed the weather changing at the top of the canyon. In fact, it looked like a blizzard. The top of the canyon was pure white. We had supplies for only eight days so we didn't have much choice but to follow our plan. It was hard to know what the snow conditions would really be like. All we know was what we could see. Maybe we should have waited a day and just ration out the remains of the food, but we decided to climb out.

Half way up we began to walk in snow. I noticed hikers coming down with crampons attached to the soles of their shoes. That was not a good sign of what was to come and how much snow and ice might really be ahead of us. The trail became a horseshoe and after the second or third turn we came to a ledge that was very narrow, in fact so narrow that I had to get down on my hands and knees and crawl. I felt so scared I could feel my heart beating louder and faster in my chest. I could feel my knees slipping and sliding underneath as I very carefully and slowly made my way one leg at a time on all fours on the ice. What a responsibility I felt. I found myself praying and visualizing all of us safe at the top. I have never felt as relieved as I did when we finally reached our destination. In fact, there was a whole group of people cheering us as we climbed over the last rock or ledge out into the Grand Canyon parking lot. I felt like kissing the ground.

Thereafter, as the expedition progressed, so did the weather worsen. I became progressively negative as the weather got worse.

I felt exhausted and on a couple of occasions, I lost it with the students for no reason. Everything got to me. I was complaining all the time about everything. It's too cold. The food is awful. I blamed my age. I blamed others, I blamed the weather, and I blamed our itinerary. You name it, I blamed.

So one day in our morning meeting with two weeks to go, I announced that I thought it best that I leave the expedition and return home. This was extremely hard for me. I felt inadequate and even ashamed. And though I had complete confidence in Nancy to lead and lead well, I also felt guilty. After all, what might this say about me?

In fact, though, the group completely supported me in my decision, and the next day I was on a bus heading back to New England. Maybe I had done something courageous in acknowledging my limits, and was not irresponsible, after all.

Bruce met me at the station in White River Junction. I hadn't seen him in nearly five weeks and I felt excitement run through me when I saw him standing there in his working jeans and outdoor boots and his long wavy hair and ever so handsome rugged and youthful face.

Though I had wondered what his reaction might be to my change of plans and early arrival, on the 45 minute drive back to the school we didn't discuss why I was here. Instead, true to Bruce's form, he instead talked with enthusiasm about his maple sugaring. Because all the students were away either on one of four expeditions or else pursuing independent internship projects, Bruce, except for making periodic visits to those with internships to check their progress and evaluate their experiences with them, had had plenty of time for one of his favorite activities, and he needed no prompting to share this as a way of reconnecting.

For my part, I actually liked just listening to him. In a way I felt relieved and reassured that even though Bruce and I often worked independently of one another while school was in session, when we did have such moments as this, I was grateful for his ability to stay focused in the present and find his own way to make it safe for both of us to take a break from the subtle drain which all of the BRS group processing could create on my reserves.

Perhaps, after all, I had not realized how much I had pushed myself to my limits and actually had a "student" experience. Now it meant much to me to be able to leave self-assessment and self-doubts aside, and just be.

Southwest expedition 1983

The expedition at Weaver's Needle

Betsy and Nancy reach the rim of the Grand Canyon

Chapter Thirteen

MUSIC, CREATIVITY, AND FUN

Music played a major part in our community. I think music drew us closer together as a community, perhaps more than anything else. Every day we sang. We opened every weekday morning meeting with singing. At first the singing looked to the students to be a bit corny, very unteen, the selections uncool, something you wouldn't want your friends back home to catch you doing. Although morning meeting was required for every student to attend, of course singing could not be required. Yet singing increased during the course of each year, and by our final year just about everyone could be heard, even pretty much from the beginning of the year. We also developed our own song book, as well as using such collections as Peter Blood's *Rise Up Singing*, which contained a great variety of genres from folk to rock, silly songs to rounds, classic hymns and gospel to historic political and union songs – all complete with chords so they could easily be "faked" on the guitar or piano. There was something for everyone.

I had grown up with little music in the house other than the 78 RPM records which I would buy in music stores. I would play the songs of my favorites like Frank Sinatra or Perry Como on my small toy-like record player in my room. This was typical of most of my friends. Music was something popular bands and singers recorded and we bought.

In retrospect, this neglect of our own singing (except for organized school glee club) was consistent with the dismissal of performance in my own family. I remember hearing that my mother had had a very beautiful voice as a young woman before she was married. My aunt used to tell us stories about how my mother performed "Danny Boy" for different groups. And yet I never heard her sing a note. Oh, how I would have loved to hear a lullaby sung by her!

As for music beyond the records, my sisters and I were for a time given weekly piano lessons on our grand piano in the living room by a teacher whose name I have never forgotten, Minnie Coon Freeman. She was no fun, had not an ounce of creativity, and had no idea how to teach children. She was of small build and wore a funny little hat. Minnie travelled the neighborhood one day a week going from house to house to give lessons to the children. I think it was just expected that all children should take piano lessons regardless of the teacher. The underlying theme in our family, however, was that we were not a musical family so it wouldn't be expected that we would take lessons beyond a customary two years. That is what happened. In fact, maybe we didn't get even that far.

Also, in fourth grade, I took up the violin but that didn't last long either. I had to put up with a lot of teasing from my sisters. People thought my playing was funny so I never took music seriously and told myself I wasn't musical anyway. That had been the family message: We just aren't a musical family. I couldn't even sing.

Actually, reclaiming music as a part of my life had begun with Re-evaluation Counseling weekend workshops. Every Friday night of these weekends was given to music, with the goal of reclaiming our creativity, of which music was such a strong component. Everyone in attendance was encouraged to get up in front of the whole workshop and sing solo. If tears and fears were aroused, crying was acceptable.

Because most of us at these workshops understood how important music was to our being alive, most people joined in the effort to reclaim their voices. For those where this was too large an assignment, they could bring three or four people up front with them and they could all sing whatever song the singer had chosen as a group. Each time I took my turn it was truly an amazing experience, and the more I challenged my fear of performance and heard the voice inside tell me I was "not musical", the louder I sang and the more I reclaimed my voice and the musician inside of me.

So by the time BRS started, I had already seen that music was potentially important in everyone's life and not just those with the beautiful voices and perfect pitch. Yet I was equally aware of how many of us have had this potential denied because we have been told we couldn't sing, not because we couldn't sing, but because our voices were judged as good or bad. After all, children sing from their soul, not from their inner critic, and the soul quite frankly doesn't care what you sound like. A singing voice ignites our energy, our aliveness and connects us to ourselves and each other. Singing is healthy in all respects. Singing is our god-given right! That much I already had learned.

In a 1983 journal entry, Bruce expressed our vision eloquently:

> Humans need the self appreciation which comes with recognizing the functioning of the brain for its creativity, its elegance, and its astounding versatility. We don't need to learn how to think or feel. Guidance and encouragement, yes. But our physical, psychological development, when not interfered with, ultimately takes care of itself. We need to clean out the garbage of hurt, distorted messages of not being enough, of self put-downs accumulated since birth, especially in our schooling and families so that such elegant functioning can actually occur all the time, not be blocked.

We applied this theory not just to academics and community building and the dynamics of expeditions, but to singing and playing musical instruments, and to performing.

Music caught on like a fever and one of those people most responsible for that was Deborah Stuart, our musical inspiration, who taught us singing and guitar, and led the community in our Christmas pageant and other musical events. Deborah lived in Wentworth with her two daughters and three sons, one of whom graduated from BRS. She was our stimulus and motivator. A guitar and autoharp player, she was enthusiastic, knew and loved music of many genres, and loved teaching us to sing and play music. Students learned from her easily. She was a gift to our community as was her music. She and her performance partner David Colburn not only performed at the school; they were also responsible for bringing other performers to our community music nights. Through their contacts we were able to bring noted folk guitarist and singer Bill Staines and the duet team of LaPlante and Pounds to the school.

The music we learned spoke of subjects and values we shared and taught at BRS: songs of hope, of dreams and fantasies. Songs about creativity, of weavers, fiddlers, dancers; songs about change, time, growing, and stages of living; songs about the rich and the poor; songs about freedom, friendship and love; songs about struggle and social change; songs about the forests, the seasons, and weather ; spiritual songs; songs about men and women.

It was also heartening personally as a parent to see Sam as a student connect with music and performance. Prior to BRS, Sam had never showed any apparent interest in any musical instrument and in fact would get very annoyed when he heard his sisters singing. One afternoon he really surprised me. I happened to be walking through the common room from the kitchen to the porch, and my eyes caught a glimpse of him holding a guitar in his lap. I don't think he even noticed me walking through the room. He was sitting on the floor with his back to me. He was bent over with a chord book in front of him figuring out where to put his fingers for each chord. I never said a word, but my whole body was jumping with joy. From that day on, I don't think a day went by without seeing him playing his guitar. And that was the way music was for many students.

In our third or fourth year we asked every staff member to take up an instrument whether we were reclaiming an instrument from our childhoods or an instrument we had never played and always wanted to play. We wanted to model something for the students. I bought a forty-five dollar fiddle at a music shop in Plymouth. I had an inner judge that rated me as "terrible", but my soul loved to hear me play and I would practice alone in my room every morning before meeting time. I was surprised how much I remembered from fourth grade. I never played in front of anyone else but I loved to play. Fifteen years later, I took up Swedish fiddle again and played with a small group of fiddlers in Washington State.

Other staff took up guitar, banjo and the piano. Bruce played the piano that was tucked into the corner of the common room, and I loved watching him tap his feet on the floor to the beat of each tune. Whenever he wasn't repairing doors or paying bills or teaching classes, he could be found leafing through song anthologies and fake books and playing the piano.

BRS was also about having fun and nurturing fun in all of us. We had skit nights and music nights with students and staff performing and always receiving rousing applause no matter how silly the skits or how elementary the music sounded. Skit nights brought out the humor in all of us. For many, performing in front of an audience took courage.

We also had such diversions as movie nights in Plymouth or Hanover, contra dancing in several Vermont and New Hampshire town halls and churches, roller skating trips to Enfield, and some day trips to Tenney Mountain for downhill skiing.

Singing with Deborah

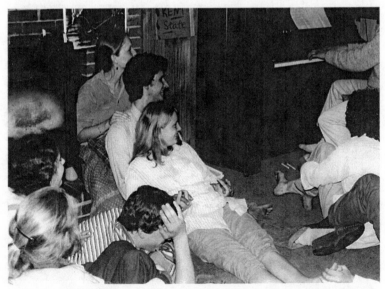

Music and creativity night in the common roon

Enjoying the music and creativity

Bruce at the piano

Chapter Fourteen

PARENTS WEEKEND

Every year, we arranged a weekend for parents and every year was in some ways different from the year before. The very first year, the weekend included both parents and students. The last four years, we sent the students home and spent the weekend only with the parents.

The first year something remarkable happened at the last event of the weekend. We had no graduates that year, but we did invite families to the school for a formal closing. As part of this event, we created two circles in the common room, an inner circle in which all the parents sat together and an outer circle where the students sat circled around their parents. As the talking stick passed around the outer circle from one student to the next, each shared something specific or in general that she or he appreciated about his parent. The impact on the parents came as a huge surprise to all of us. One by one each parent seemed so moved by the appreciation that the words brought tears. Soon there was much crying and laughter.

Then we switched and the parents, facing their child told him or her specifically what they loved about them. The students began to cry also. I think everyone was surprised at how intense appreciations could be and how they go to the core of who we are and how connecting and important appreciations and validations are to the bonding between parents and children.

I remember especially the parent's weekend in 1983 as a good example of the night-and-day difference of this event from typical school parents' weekends.

For this event, all students left for the weekend so that it was a parents-only event. No sooner had we said good-bye to our students that late Friday afternoon than we found ourselves greeting a new batch of students – their parents. In our morning meeting earlier in the day, before the students left, we had shared with them the agenda for the weekend: Saturday was to be very much like a regular day at school. The parents would be signing up for kitchen crew jobs of cooking and cleaning up, daily chores. The day would begin with breakfast followed by morning meeting and singing. "Go no further!" jumped in one student when she heard the word "sing". "There is no way my parents are going to be singing. I have never heard them sing." Others chimed in also with the same reaction. And one added, "And don't do skits."

It was obvious that some of the students whose parents had never spent any time here at school other than to drop them off after a vacation were nervous about how their mom or dad would react. They perhaps remembered their first impression and how different this kind of community felt to them and I guess they also felt somewhat possessive of what they had and feared what might happen if their parents were to criticize and make fun of some of the happenings which even felt weird to them when first experienced. We tried our best to reassure them and let them know we understood how they were feeling, that it made sense they wouldn't want their parents to freak out - and the implications of that for them. We hoped they would understand that the purpose for this weekend was to have parents experience the school for themselves from the inside out and to better understand the school and its philosophy around learning and also to help them to better understand adolescence, maybe their own as well as their child's.

The twenty parents who had signed up for the weekend arrived, some with and some without spouses, hopeful, maybe a bit anxious, about the weekend and what would be expected of them. Here was their first experience as students.

First, some explanation. Everyone entering the Yellow House had to go through the mud room, a long narrow unheated space with an unfinished cement floor, and outside doors at either end plus two small half bathrooms off the entry. The mud room connected the outdoors to the main part of the Yellow House. On one side of the wall in the mud room, we had built forty good sized cubbies. Each student and staff member was assigned a cubby where they could store their outside boots shoes and other items like scarves, gloves, and hats before entering. Doing this insured that we could keep all the floors inside the house free of all the mud, debris, and wet from the outside and especially protect our common room carpet where we all sat.

We directed the arriving parents to their own student's cubby, and this first step worked really well. The parents had no problem with taking off their "outside" shoes and putting them into their son or daughter's cubby. Parents had been previously notified about bringing slippers or something for indoor use only and some of the parents were even greeted with comfy slippers supplied by their student.

So far, so good. Friday night after dinner we met in the common room. Except for a few bad backs and arthritic knees, everyone seemed willing and able to relax onto the cushy carpet in the common room, some resting against the many pillows just as their kids did every day. We each introduced ourselves, told where we were from and what our expectations and hopes were for the weekend.

Following that we introduced those silly mixer games some of the students were afraid would turn off their parents. If we deserve credit for any of our thinking and planning about the weekend, we earned it for having the courage to introduce parents to "silly" games in spite of the student's fears. Students seemed to be out of touch with the playfulness of their parents. Life maybe at home had become too serious. But the parents played and laughed just as hard if not harder than their kids. I think the laughing and playfulness really relaxed them.

Then we went over the rules and policies and answered questions. We passed around the room the signup sheets for cook and cleanup for the next five meals. Parents willingly signed up. Some parents stayed up late to talk and connect with other parents. I went to bed early.

Saturday morning breakfast was served promptly at 7 a.m. I loved hearing the parents joking with each other in the kitchen as they cut up fruit, and made the muffins from scratch.

Before morning meeting officially began, we introduced the other most feared event expressed by the students and that was our singing. Margie, one of our staff, handed out the song books and from the enthusiasm parents showed for singing, I knew we were off to a good start. I taped their singing so that on Monday morning when the students were back I could play back their voices. I think they were later amazed to hear their parents' enthusiasm.

After the singing we moved into the main part of the weekend which was to talk about and experience the BRS education. Using our talking stick, we went around the room giving each parent the opportunity to share something positive about their own learning. The second time around they shared something negative.

The discussion for the morning evolved out of the contents of Marilyn Ferguson's fairly recent book *The Aquarian Conspiracy* and her identification and fresh understandings of new and old paradigms for learning. Our staff had often previously used this book as a frame of reference for looking at what we were doing as a school and community, because her thoughts resonated with the assumptions and goals we had for BRS. In the book, she describes the overall paradigm of learning in this way:

The larger paradigm looks to the nature of learning rather than methods of instruction. Learning after all is not schools, teachers, literacy, math, grades, and achievement. It is the process by which we have moved every step of the way since we first breathed; the transformation that occurs in the brain whenever new information is integrated whenever a new skill is mastered. Learning is kindled in the mind of the individual. Anything else is mere schooling.

What followed as we covered each of the below topics was a very lively "class" with very eager students.

We discussed the five paradigms that the vision of the school rested on, stressing difference from typical paradigms which focused on achieving certain norms for learning as reflected in test scores, being obedient, and providing correct answers. The new paradigms, we explained, pointed to the importance of asking questions and motivating lifelong learning, strengthening self discipline, awakening curiosity, and encouraging creative risk-taking in all people. We discussed how we as a school were implementing those ideas through insisting that there was no such thing as a stupid question and requiring that all projects undertaken each module involved seeking an answer to a significant question that with staff guidance they had chosen.

We also discussed the need to understand feelings so that when separated out from thoughts, students could make appropriate decisions and choices. Again we talked about our emotionally illiterate culture and how that disconnected us from the past. Without that understanding of the past, we are all likely to continue to act on "not mattering", "not being important", "not being loveable" or "being inadequate/ stupid". Our lives simply remain stuck in those unconscious feelings.

We talked about the theory of Re-evaluation Counseling and how we used that as a tool for teaching students to feel safe expressing their feelings as a means to getting underneath to the thoughts. Under every negative acting-out child was a hurt child.

We talked and answered questions about our seven-week expeditions that began first part of March and that at various times gone as far north as the Canadian border, as far west as the California desert, and as far south as Florida and the Mexican border, and, in the case of one particular expedition, into the heart of Mexico.

We explained and discussed our encouragement for everyone to take up a musical instrument, not in order to become a performer, but for the joy of playing music. The result was that we had people playing guitar, banjo, flute, piano, autoharp, and violin. We described our music nights where students could entertain if they wished, noting the thunderous applause not necessarily for proficiency but for the act of getting up in from of a group and being noticed. Doing that enriched self esteem and self importance.

Then we divided into groups with each group assigned to go off and make up a skit illustrating some piece of the contrast between the old and new paradigms to show an aspect of their own school experience and then how they would have liked it to be. For many, this proved to be the first time they had really thought about their own education much less thinking about what they thought about learning in general and in particular. They were challenged by this assignment as well as in making a connection between their experiences and how they parented their children.

The skits and the processing of them took up the rest of the morning, but discussion between them continued for the rest of the day, in the kitchen preparing lunch and cleaning up. In the afternoon, many of the parents walked up and down the hill or around the property. Some helped out in the fields to lend a hand to the ongoing work of the wood crew. We had to get our twenty-two cords of wood in for the following season, and much had yet to be moved and stacked. Others met in the common room and continued their discussions or some just took it easy and napped.

We came together again as a group at dinnertime. I noticed there seemed to be so much more cohesion. After dinner, we had two folk singers entertain us. They were old favorites who had been up to the school many times before and they happened to be touring in the area. The evening was fun and relaxed.

On Sunday morning after breakfast we chose the topic of parenting and started off the discussion quoting this from Dr Thomas Gordon, founder of Parent Effectiveness Training:

> Parents do the best they can with the little if no training provided to them for the job of parenting. You tell me another job that has more importance than the job of parenting. But we have this stereotype idea that you don't need training for parenting, that it comes naturally and all you have to do is love your child, provide him/ her with the right kind of things, and s/he will automatically grow into a healthy person and the relationship will be a satisfactory one.

> But we know this is not true. Parents are doing the best they can but that is not good enough. As a matter of fact, I don't think we have changed our method of raising children for 2000 years. Basically, parents use power and authority to resolve conflicts, and they have been doing this for years. Parents use their power to get their needs met at the expense of the child not getting his or hers met.

Parents responded to this and shared their frustrations of trying to protect their children and in the process inadvertently trying to manage and control their lives and decisions. They described worrying about losing them, which prevented them from seeing their children's strengths and building strengths. They talked about finding themselves judging and evaluating each performance, academic, creative or personal for failure or success and then giving advice or criticism when not solicited. Some acknowledged their acting out feelings of anger, or fear with their children, openly sharing family scenes of hysteria, pleas, and endless rehearsal of "scripts."; and then at times feeling guilty and apologizing for being a failure and never doing enough as a parent. And they also acknowledged creating too much of a laissez-faire environment with not enough limits or boundary-setting or enough responsibilities.

We appreciated their honesty and openness, and as a parent I could understand and validate everything they were saying. I noted that in order to teach at most levels, including secondary, one needed at least a BA degree and in some places an MA in teaching. To be a parent you need nothing. However, effective parenting and meeting all the emotional and physical, mental, spiritual needs of a child require the equivalent of a Ph.D. And although that sounds impossible, parents need at least some training.

One parent said at the close of the weekend when we were sharing what was valuable about the weekend, "I love coming here because I always learn something new. It doesn't always hit me right away but when it does it makes a difference in the way I act at home and in my job. And I love meeting other parents."

One of the dads expressed it this way: "I'm more at home working with computers than I am with people, but it has been a high point meeting parents and staff and seeing the feelings the kids share and the way staff love them."

A staff member shared, "The community is twice as big as I thought it was because there's a whole part I hadn't seen until now. I realize you are just as much a part of this community as anyone else here. Your input and ideas are essential."

We learned from our weekends that parents did not want to be treated as guests. They coveted understanding about the school that their children talked and wrote about so much. Through their participation in the weekend and their questions, parents explored every nook and cranny of the school's philosophy and how it applied to their children and their everyday life on the hill. They wanted to know its implications for them and for their relationships at home. Developing skills of active listening and conflict resolution; learning to express love more openly and frequently; granting permission to feel; knowing that they are not alone; the insight that beyond our own feelings is an accurate and appropriate response to every situation, crisis or routine. These were for parents some of the useful outcomes from the weekend.

Our experience interacting with the parents also later led our staff to reflect on what we were doing on a broader philosophical scale as a daunting project of contradicting student low self-esteem.

Having seen during the weekend that their parents carried low esteem, we had been reminded that our students' feelings of loneliness, isolation, unimportance, and unworthiness, all of which comprise low self-esteem, were in many ways simply a re-enactment of what they had learned and come to believe from their parents. It was only a short step from there to surmise that their parents' low self esteem in turn had its source in their parents' own experience as children growing up in their families.

So it became clearer than ever that low self-esteem should be treated with the same sense of urgency as a threatening medical disease, a virus which if unchecked passes on from one generation to the next. If we don't interrupt the patterns in our children, we will be faced with the virus in the form of the next generation of well intentioned but uninformed parents.

So in a way we were reaffirmed in our mission and the urgency of what we were doing, especially since the predominant educational paradigm seems so sacredly attached to an educational system more attuned to the needs of the economy than to the needs of a society of whole. To sum it all up, our goal was to develop fulfilled, loving human beings, whose success is measured not on how much money they make but on the quality of their relationship with self, a relationship which becomes reflected in their relationship with family, friends, community and ultimately the world.

PART 4:

THE CLOSING OF BAKER RIVER SCHOOL

Chapter One

THE DECISION TO CLOSE

Because the last year of Baker River School in 1983 was so successful, people may wonder why we chose to close the school. The answer was quite simple: our physical facilities were, despite our improvements and ingenious adaptations, absolutely minimal. The salaries and living arrangements for staff were definitely not adequate to keep our young teachers for any extended period – love the work, the program, and the students as they might. To provide adequate facilities, first by thoroughly renovating the barn into a multipurpose facility, then by building staff housing, would cost by our estimate at least $330,000—an amount almost twice the school's annual budget (the staff in 1982-83 was earning $4000 per year plus room and board, usually living in single rooms in the midst of students). The needed money was not to be found among our constituents, supportive and enthusiastic they were. And our small voice was not to be heard among the clamorous competition for grants for foundations or businesses, even when we found the time for any development work, especially in the time of an economic recession.

As Co-Directors, Bruce and I felt personally that we could not continue for another year under fixed circumstances which held no promise for change as far as we could see. Beside the above considerations, we were graduating 10 of our 23 students, and admissions for the fall were very slim. This was a very sad time, especially for returning students who had hopes of graduating from BRS and staff who saw this teaching environment as what they had dreamed of in becoming teachers.

There was some irony in the situation, for we had experienced success, real qualitative growth. We had learned, we were continuing to learn, we were implementing what we were learning. Our last year was by all accounts the best one. But after all, the school had been conceived as an experiment, not a personal monument to posterity. And while it may be romantic to read into the passage of events some over-riding cosmic intention, we were clear, as we looked back on our experience, that indeed things did work out for the best. We had created one microcosm of what a saner, safer, more energized, and more connected community might look like, and one where great challenges stimulated rewarding growth.

At the time of the closing a local Plymouth newspaper wrote, in part:

> Educational institutions over the years have struggled to improve the learning process. BRS has seen the emotional and human side of learning as having been the least explored in the learning process. The effects of personal crisis eventually surface if not in high school or college classrooms, then later in family life or the work place. Students learned skills to help each other and to help themselves. They learned not only how to listen to each other and to become comfortable with each others anger, grief, and joy. "They taught us how to listen to them", reported one staff member.

> Equally important was for the adults to learn to discipline their use of power and authority not to control young people, but to set the limits that make personal and academic growth possible. Such limit setting is an act of caring. The

use and abuse of drugs in our schools and families is a symptom of people not learning to communicate everyday problems and emotions. Honest and healthy communication does not happen when drugs are present. From the beginning, the founders were determined to have a community where there were no drugs at all—for both students and staff. This did not happen without a struggle on the part of the entire school community. Some students left BRS when they realized drug use was not being swept under the rug. One of the signs of success this year has been that students have monitored their own and each other's behavior concerning drugs.

And finally, BRS sends this year's graduating class of ten out to join former graduates at such colleges as Wheelock College, University of Massachusetts, University of Wisconsin, Clark University, and Hampshire College.

School picture 1983

Staff 1982-1983

Betsy and Bruce at Graduation 1983

BETSY BERGQUIST

Graduation 1983

Chapter Two

BRUCE'S FINAL GRADUATION ADDRESS

At the 1983 graduation, Bruce put voice to our feelings about the school and its closing as follows:

> When one gets to the end of an experience like ours of the last six years and then is asked to conclude it with a talk of ten minutes, my first thought is that there is no way that anything appropriate can be condensed into that time.
>
> In my case, though, when I sat down to put something to paper I couldn't at first think of anything to say. I'm happy to report though that my old English teacher's instincts soon proved still intact. And feelings and thoughts began to come in abundance. The problem after all was one of condensation so those of you who want the full scoop will have to await our book. I will be brief.
>
> First of all, to all of you who have been students here - alumni, graduates, today and former and present students:

This has been an outstanding and unique school, and the fact that it is closing doesn't in any way devalue your educational experience here.

This goes especially for what you've learned about your feelings, about the sources of conflict and pain in the world, and how it's been passed from parents to children, one generation to the next, also about what you've learned about loving yourself fully and without reservation as the basis for cooperating with and loving others and the world around you.

What you've learned about anger, sadness, fear and joy, love, zest is knowledge for all seasons.

It goes too for what you've learned about learning - how to ask questions, how to go about getting answers, how to sense the reliability of the information you come upon. There is nothing more valuable than useful tools in a world of officialdom and media hype.

It goes too for what you've learned about the world today and role as US citizens. Value these insights, your thinking and information. Don't be put off if you're challenged by others - especially older people - or if you are not always correct or complete or on target with your information. Feel, mad, feel scared, sure, but then keep your focus on getting yourself informed. Be proud to be an American - thinking, questioning, and loving, skeptical, patriotic American. The world does not need, on one hand, either smug, chauvinistic, Americans or on the other hand, Americans so overwhelmed by anger and guilt about their country that they can't think constructively about what needs to be done here or elsewhere.

To Parents:

Thank you for sharing your children with us. We have all learned together. Like you we have alternately felt puzzled, exasperated, uplifted, devastated and – at moments too precious to forget- absolutely astonished and exhilarated by their brilliance and creativity. We are tired now and need rest but I would not give back one moment of the past six years - would not choose to erase even the most painful memory of the most difficult student in the most difficult situation. Thank you also, parents, for your example of openness and receptivity to change. I daresay that if the world was populated by parents like you, it would be by far a safer, warmer, more loving place. And schools such as ours would be flourishing everywhere. Finally, you've told us that your children have seen to it that the values of BRS get tested at home. I trust this will continue to happen. The school lives on through their spirit and example.

To Friends

Don't feel sad or hopeless or even worse, guilty today. Your generosity of thought and action has kept us going. We may be as broke now as when we started, but without your help we would have been flat busted years ago. There's not an inch of this place that isn't occupied by something borrowed from or donated by or bought by through the gift of a friend. You have only to look around the school. There's no way I could recount all of your favors and gifts both small and large. Make your own tally right now if you wish and appreciate yourself for what you did and know that we feel likewise. It isn't anyone's fault that none of you had the pile of money to pay salaries or build facilities we would have needed to think about continuing.

To Staff:

You can justifiably feel you've learned as much as the students. The wisdom and management of skills of listening, of consensus-reaching, of knowing how to challenge and support yourself and others, of combating oppression, of peacemaking are already yours. You can't escape them, so you will be using them. And you are in demand: witness the fact that just a few weeks ago when we decided to close the school, most of you already have new jobs or solid prospects for them. And in places where your experience will make an immediate decisive difference. With love and appreciation I take from BRS your example of caring, persisting, and cooperating. We really did this together.

Finally, for everyone:

When the trustees made their decision a few weeks ago to close the school, we prepared and sent a letter of explanation to our many friends. Many of you have seen the letter. We have already received some replies and I would like to read one of them. It's from our friend Helen Brooks over in Woodstock, Vermont. She is 84 years old and one of Betsy's mother's dearest friends.

Although Betsy and I appreciate her kind words about us in the letter, that's not why I'm reading it. I'm reading it because it embodies such fine spirit and conveys such a correct and appropriate tone to be adopted under the present world circumstances - circumstances which in a way are mirrored (in feeling at least) by what has happened at BRS.

Dear Betsy and Bruce:

It was with more than a twinge of nostalgia that I read your letter of May 25. While I knew that you never meant Baker River School to be your life work it is hard to realize that so much has been accomplished in so short a time. The fact that you did it during a very bad recession is remarkable and I know that the fortunate students who were under your teaching and a part of your far reaching programs will be influenced all their lives by their experiences.

With the growth of the peace movement and a need for retreats I can see hundreds of people responding to the beauty and quiet of your location. Do pursue this and I shall spread the word around here when I hear more. We are going to Weston on June 11 to meditate and pray with the brothers at the Priory – they expect 1000. Last Saturday we had a two hour peace Vigil at St. James with eight speakers from different faiths. And my 81 year old brother who is bicycling all over Europe has addresses from the International Fellowship of Reconciliation to which he will bring messages from San Jose. Something good must come out of this.

To you my dear young friends, I shall always be interested in where you are and what you are doing. You are one of my strongest reasons for hope in this crazy world so keep in touch and start climbing to the next station.

Devotedly, Helen

Helen's tone is one of firm hope, no-nonsense pragmatism, spiritual confidence, and expectation of good things from other people (in this case, us). This is a letter I'm planning to keep. And assuming that no one here today has yet reached 84 I suggest that Helen Brooks' directive to climb to the next station is an apt call for all of us younger than she as we take our leave from this place.

PS And by the way, she lived to be nearly 108!

Our family at Bruce's 50th 1983

My Life after Baker River School

Having reclaimed my love and strong desire to learn, and with encouragement and support from Bruce, a year after the closing of BRS I enrolled in the MALS (Master of Arts in Liberal Studies) program at Dartmouth College and graduated in 1988. Bruce and I moved to the state of Washington in 1989. There, with a strong curiosity to learn more about me and my potential, and with a motivation to develop a career for myself, I enrolled in Antioch Seattle University's MA in Psychology program and graduated in 1991. After my graduation, and having begun my private practice as a mental health counselor, I became painfully aware, and Bruce concurred, that our relationship needed some help. We just happened to see the author and couples' counselor Harville Hendrix Ph.D. on public television conducting a couples' workshop entitled "Getting the Love You Want", based on what he termed Imago Relationship Therapy. It really spoke to our needs and led to the next step in our growth as a couple.

After attending the workshop and learning more about our style of communication, we in earnest began at our work to "get what we wanted" in our relationship. I also became a certified Imago therapist as well as a couples' workshop presenter.

Since then, in addition to continuing my private practice, I have with Bruce presented over 85 "Getting the Love You Want" weekend workshops which we currently offer in New Jersey and Massachusetts. Having become even more extensive historians of our own childhoods and understanding the hurts and beliefs that controlled much of our lives, Bruce and I have learned how we were both part of the problem in our communication and have come far in creating a relationship based on appreciation and care.

My emphasis with couples has in some ways been an extension of where I was headed at Baker River School. I seek to help them see that the emotional needs that weren't met in their childhoods and how they adapted to those unmet needs as well as nurture some of the emotional, mental, creative, assertive parts of themselves that they had to put aside/give up/disown in order to receive love and acceptance from their parents are now surfacing in the relationship.

Baker River School 2007 Reunion

I had already started writing this book by mid-2007, yet it might not have come to full fruition without the inspiration, encouragement and motivation provided by a reunion organized that summer by several former students and staff, Bruce and me.

I had certainly at that time not forgotten how profound an experience it was for me as well as its extraordinary impact on all the students and staff. But the more I wrote, the more I wanted to connect with the students and staff again. And I found out many of them felt the same way.

So on a weekend in late August 2007, about 20 former students and staff, plus assorted family members, gathered from as far away as the West Coast and Russia at Woolman Hill, a conference center near Deerfield, Massachusetts, a facility that came as close to replicating the BRS environment as we could find. Many of us had not seen each other for 20 years or more. Sam, now 44 years old, was there with his wife and two young sons. He had graduated from

Hampshire College in 1987 and later earned his MA in teaching from Lesley University. Now, he was about to return for his 14th year of teaching elementary school. Besides teaching, one of his continued passions was his music which he not only brought to his classroom experience but to Boston Loose Change, a band that he had helped to organize. Of course, he brought his music with him to the reunion.

After a Friday evening of dinner and socializing including families, we began Saturday with a morning meeting. We actually remembered and sang many of the songs we used to sing.

Then we devoted much of the morning to finding out from everyone how the school impacted them and what they still carried with them. Besides hearing both brief and not-so-brief stories about far-flung adventures and accomplishments (which were most heartening in themselves, and often very funny) from everyone, here are some of the most significant comments about the BRS experience that I recall hearing:

> You all became my family. At BRS I was asked to be open and vulnerable. The culture doesn't ask that of us. We learned a new language of feelings so when I left, it was tough for me because there was no one to talk to in that same way. Often I had to figure out a way to close down and not be vulnerable.

> The heart of the school was that everyone was good and we were given permission to believe that. The society focuses on our behavior as an indication of our goodness but here everyone was good regardless.

> Coming to the school I couldn't really appreciate the impact I had on other people. I didn't understand my importance or value to others either good or bad. There, I was beginning to understand that.

Most of the staff (except for Betsy and Bruce) were in their twenties. How much responsibility they had and how much they were trusted!

What was the most difficult was, having learned and experienced this sense of community, when I left the school how disconnected I felt going back into the real world. I think many of us felt terribly alone and maybe even resentful that there was no preparation to make the transition back into the emotionally distant "real" world.

I learned how important community was and how dependent everyone was on each other. If one person screwed up how that affected everyone else. Also, every voice mattered.

Telling the truth in the community was such a radical thing to do. Saying what I felt was scary but that afterwards I would feel so much more a part of the community when I had shared her truth.

I realized that what back then may have seemed somewhat mundane like walking up the hill in the dark, or singing in morning meeting, or even speaking out in community meetings really did stretch me in acting against beliefs of not belonging, or not mattering or being important, or feeling limited, and instead deepened my feeling of connection and having value.

In addition to student comments, staff members also talked, in particular about how much they learned about their own adolescence as well as simply the importance of relationships, noting that they often felt more like co-learners and students themselves.

In true BRS spirit, the rest of the weekend included tending to the food and cleanup by the group, a scintillating music and performance night, and a spontaneous group swim in the Deerfield River, complete with rope-swinging from a formidable height. We left with full intention to do it again.

So in reflecting on the reunion experience, it seemed far more like BRS itself than a typical reunion. The spirit, connection, and sense of community and fun have not been lost, nor are they just memories.